MYSTICS AND MATTER

"The science behind Indian spirituality"

Preetam Ku Pradhan

REDGRAB books
redgrabbooks.com

RG
books

Published By

Redgrab Books Pvt. Ltd.

942, Mutthiganj, Prayagraj, 211003

www.redgrabbooks.com

contact@redgrabbooks.com

Price in India : 250/- INR

First published by Redgrab Books in 2024

Printed and bound in India

Cover Design & Typesetting by Redgrab Books team

ISBN : 978-93-95697-91-0

"Hare Krishna Hare Krishna, Krishna Krishna Hare Hare

Hare Rama Hare Rama , Rama Rama Hare Hare"

ACKNOWLEDGEMENT

I am deeply grateful for the journey that has culminated in the publication of this book. First and foremost, my heartfelt thanks to *Redgrab Publications* for believing in this work and bringing it to life, and to *The Book Bakers*, whose literary guidance and representation were invaluable.

This book would not have been possible without the unwavering support of my parents and family members, whose encouragement has been my constant source of strength. I am especially indebted to *Shri Achyuta Samanta*, Founder of *KIIT* and *KISS*, for his blessings, which have been a profound inspiration throughout this endeavor. I am also sincerely grateful to *Bhavani Prasad Panda Sir*, former Director of Law Prof. (Dr.) Rose Varghese Director, KIIT School of Law Formerly, Vice-Chancellor, National Law University (NUALS, Kochi) and *Faiz Ayat Ansari* Sir, Assistant Professor of law whose mentorship helped shape my understanding and vision.

A special note of appreciation goes to my professors at *KIIT School of Law*, whose knowledge and guidance have been instrumental in refining my thoughts and ideas.

To everyone who played a role in this journey—thank you for your invaluable support and encouragement. This book is a tribute to all of you.

ABSTRACT

Philosophers, theologians and physicists have all discussed the issue of God's ultimate existence for ages. While some maintain that there is no physical evidence to back such a notion, others counter that the complexity and order of the cosmos hint to the existence of an intelligent creator.

The existence of God is ultimately a matter of personal belief, and each person must come to their own conclusions based on their unique experiences and viewpoints. While some people may find solace and meaning in their faith in God, others can believe that the cosmos is essentially random and without significance. The existence of God is still ultimately a mystery that each person must approach in their own way.

In this book, the author tries to find the answer of difficult, undiscovered, spiritual questions that remain unanswered century after century. The author tries to prove the existence of god and maintains balance between devotion and science in the contemporary world of lifestyle.

Research Questions

There are many spiritual reasonable questions like, who is God? Does God really exist? If yes, why no one has seen God till now? What is the nature of God? What is the law of karma? Did God create this universe? Is there any scientific evidence of life after death? Do spirits and souls really exist?

We will try to answer these research questions by encoding different ancient texts and codes written by ancient sages and rishis.

INTRODUCTION

Indian society is rich in its culture and heritage and one of the ancient civilisations based on scientific approach and research. Ancient Indian society is one of the most advanced in Vedic science, art and architecture.

'Arthasashtra' between 2nd century BCE and 3rd century CE by Kautalya is one of the best examples of administrative system and governance; even today, it's unconsciously incorporated in our Indian constitution. International relations and foreign affairs were strategically and tactically drafted by Acharya Chanakya. Manusmruti and Danda Shastra are one of the best legal codes of ancient India. However, some clauses are still in practice in the contemporary legal system.

Every Christian knows English and every Muslim knows Urdu. They read and understand their ancient texts in their own language. But ancient Indian texts are written in Sanskrit and the problem is that in the contemporary era, people don't know Sanskrit. There is not much scope to learn Sanskrit as this language is an optional paper.

From time to time, many scholars and researchers translated the ancient texts of Vedas, Upanishads and Puranas. The facts and information were altered, interpreted and manipulated by many translators for their own benefit. Old education Gurukul system of India was overthrown by the crown in British India.

Let's understand this with an example. We are still taught in our secondary high classes that 'Kalidas' was Shakespeare of India. But it's shocking fact that Kalidas existed 1,000 years before Shakespeare. Shouldn't Shakespeare be called the Kalidas of England? This is the finest example of western domination on our Indian education system.

Education policy framed by British is still deep rooted in our culture. Our education system does not teach leadership qualities in children but trains them to become excellent clerks to serve Your Majesty. Formal education system gives no space to creativity, skill, talent and experience. That's why everyone is in a rush for government jobs. Thus, the holy books we read are interpreted and manipulated versions of ancient texts, which contain many errors and faults.

When the British came to India, they wanted to break the culture, so they systematically engineered it and Indians forgot their own culture, acquiring and adopting western culture and lifestyle; meanwhile, the answer to the questions of life and existence remained undiscovered in ancient Vedic books, Vedas and Upanishads.

6 million Jews died in World War 2; they write and make movies about it. Nobody is supposed to forget about it in the world, everybody is reminded everyday about how these atrocities happened to them but the Bengal famine in India killed over three and half million people in a matter of three months because Britishers took away all the food and resources to fulfil World War 2.

It's recorded in British history but it's not mentioned in Indian history. If government makes schemes for people to get a free meal twice a day, they are happy. We should not ignore our history and develop animosity towards somebody but at the same time, it's stupidity to forget everything and go on like nothing has happened.

In this book, the author tries to find answers to the questions of life and origin, encoding different ancient texts and codes relative to modern science and technology.

INDEX

Chapter 1

Creator of the Creation - 13

1.1) The divine entity God. - 15

1.2) Manifestation of god and energy. - 20

1.3) Nature of God (Brahma, Vishnu and mahesh) - 27

Chapter 2

"Yoga sastra" Bio-physics analysis- - 31

2.1) Existence of spirits and soul. - 32

2.2) Feeling of Experience God and energy. - 36

2.3) How to experience god and energy - 38

Chapter3

Divine Rules of Creation- - 45

3.1) Creation of universe - 46

3.2) life after Death cycle - 53

3.3) Law of Karma . - 58

Chapter 4

Mystics and occult Science - 66

4.1) Yantra - 68

4.2) Mantra - 72

4.3) Tantra - 74

Chapter 5

Supernatural Abilities and Siddhi - 78

5.1) Analysis on Siddhi - 80

5.2) Types of siddhi - 82

5.3) how to attain siddhis - 92

Chapter 1

THE DIVINE ENTITY GOD (QUANTUM THEORY, COSMOLOGY AND METAPHYSICS)

The idea of a heavenly being or God has fascinated people and inspired reflection throughout human history. Numerous faiths and belief systems hold the concept of a greater power or force that controls the universe, and this concept has also been the focus of intellectual and scientific study. The nature of God and its relationship with the universe have recently been under the spotlight thanks to developments in quantum theory, cosmology and metaphysics. With its emphasis on the interconnectivity and entanglement of all things, quantum theory, for example, presents a drastically different perspective of the cosmos than classical physics.

Contrarily, cosmology has provided insight into the beginnings and development of the cosmos, prompting concerns regarding the presence of a supernatural creator or intelligent design. The underlying essence of reality, including the idea of a transcendent or divine reality outside of the physical world, is the subject of metaphysics, on the other hand. Together, these disciplines present a wide range of concepts and hypotheses that can shed light on God's character and position in the cosmos. Others view these ideas as a framework for examining the nature of consciousness and the human experience, while some contend that the findings of quantum theory and cosmology constitute scientific evidence for the presence of a divine being or intelligent designer.

We will explore the various concepts and theories that have developed from these domains and how they add to our understanding of the divine entity as we explore the intersection of God, quantum theory, cosmology and metaphysics in this chapter.

The author equates Bhagavad Gita, which is considered as a divine holy book with quantum theory considered as the most complex and mystical science till now. The author tries to explain the nature of god with the help of cosmology and metaphysics.

1.1 The Divine Entity God

The presence of a divine being, also known as God, has long been a source of controversy and dispute. While some say that various philosophical and theological reasons can demonstrate god's presence, others maintain that it is impossible to demonstrate or refute the existence of a divine being. We will analyse the arguments for and against the presence of a divine being as we investigate the idea of God in this book.

What Is God?

It's crucial to define what we understand by god before we examine the arguments for and against his or her existence. God is viewed differently in various religions and intellectual traditions, yet this supernatural being is frequently said to share some basic traits. God is frequently referred to as all-knowing, all-powerful and all-good. Others contend that God is transcendent, meaning that he exists outside of the material world and is incomprehensible to us. In addition, God is regarded as the creator of the entire cosmos by numerous religions and intellectual schools.

Arguments in Favour of God's Existence

There are many reasons that have been presented in favour of God's existence. The cosmological argument, the teleological argument and the moral argument are three major categories into which these arguments might be divided.

According to the cosmological hypothesis, God must have been the cause of the universe's creation. The foundation of this argument is the notion that since everything in the cosmos has a cause, the universe as a whole must also have a cause. There must be an uncaused, everlasting and necessary factor that created the universe, and this factor is sometimes identified as God.

The teleological argument, also referred to as the argument from design, asserts that the universe's complexity and orderliness indicate that an intelligent creator, primarily God, was responsible for its creation. This claim is frequently demonstrated with the use of instances like the intricacy of the human eye, which is cited as proof of intelligent design.

According to the moral argument, the world's presence of objective moral principles and obligations points to a moral lawgiver, namely God. This argument is founded on the notion that if there are objective moral principles and obligations, then these principles must have a source, and that source is frequently identified as being God.

Arguments Against the Existence of God

While there are many reasons for God's existence, there are just as many that are against it. The existence of evil, the argument from unbelief and conflicting revelations are a few of the most popular objections against the existence of God.

The most well-known objection against God's existence is perhaps the dilemma of evil. This argument contends that an all-knowing, all-powerful and all-good God cannot exist in a world where there is evil. If God is all-knowing, he would be aware of the evil in the world; if God is all-powerful, he could stop evil from happening; and if God is all-good, he would wish to stop evil. The existence of evil therefore shows that God does not.

According to the argument from non-belief, the fact that there are people who do not believe in God yet lack faith is evidence that God is not real. Everyone should have access to the proof required for belief of God is real and wants to interact with people. It suggests that God does not exist and that there are sceptics who have not been given this proof.

The existence of various and conflicting religious views shows that God does not exist, according to the argument from inconsistent revelations. There should be a single, consistent set of beliefs that appropriately depicts God's nature and character if there is one god who longs for a connection with mankind.

Analysis on the Existence of God with Ancient Texts

अहं सर्वस्य प्रभवो मत्त: सर्वं प्रवर्तते |
इति मत्वा भजन्ते मां बुधा भावसमन्विता:

"All creations originate from me. Everything commences from me. The wise who know this fact always worship me with devotion."

Krishna in Bhagavad Gita, Chapter 10:8 (Vibhuti Yog)

In *The Ancient India*, Acharya Kanada gave the theory of parmanu which was considered the simplest indestructible particle of matter. Today, modern science calls it 'atom'. It is the simplest form of a particle which forms the basis of all elements in nature.

In the modern era, with the development of science and technology, today scientists believe even the atom has the simplest particle within it. Quantum physics deals with the study of nature and behaviour of matter and energy on atomic and subatomic levels. Modern atomic scientists suggest that atoms are made up of energy. This energy, mainly negative, is termed as electron; positive energy within the atom is termed as proton; and neutral particle as neutron.

An atom consists of subatomic energy called quarks, photons and electrons which form the basis of all material elements that exist in this universe. Atoms are made of energy and therefore, we can say that energy is the basis and fundamental stone of all creation.

The ancient Vedas, Puranas and Upanishads consider energy as supreme and heavenly in nature. The energy that exists in this universe is absolute. Therefore, we can call energy as *god.*

Chapter 10, Vibhuti Yog, in the Bhagavad Gita, depicts and gives emphasis on the supreme power of energy, its nature, behaviour and existence:

न मे विदु: सुरगणा: प्रभवं न महर्षय: |
अहमादिर्हि देवानां महर्षीणां च सर्वश: || 2||

Neither celestial being nor saints know my origin. I am the source from which great saints and gods are born.

Chapter 10:2 (Vibhuti Yog)

यो मामजमनादिं च वेत्ति लोकमहेश्वरम् |
असम्मूढ: स मर्त्येषु सर्वपापै: प्रमुच्यते || 3||

I am unborn and beginningless. I am the supreme lord of the universe. Those who understand me gets free from the illusion of this world.

Chapter 10:3 (Vibhuti Yog)

In his general relativity theory, Einstein stated: “Energy can neither be created nor be destroyed.”

Even today, cosmic scientists are in search of the creation of the universe, which is hypothesised in the Big Bang theory but not yet proved.

Diversified Opinions on God

There is only one Jesus Christ and 72 sects of Christianity. One Lord Buddha and 32 sects of Buddhism. One Allah and 135 sects of Islam. In Hinduism, one can’t even count. Every sect tries to propagate that their sect is the best in the world. There exists diversity and different opinions. No harm in the existence of contradictory views. The only thing that matters is ‘karma’:

दुःख में सुमिरन सब करे सुख में करे न कोय।
जो सुख में सुमिरन करे दुःख काहे को होय ॥

Sant Kabir Das

Today, people have given God the role of an insurance agent. If something wrong happens in our life then God suddenly arises out of the emptiness of our minds; when something good happens, we forget even ourselves.

The devotees of Ram always chant ‘Ram Ram Ram’, they don’t utter a single word except Ram. When they are happy, sad, good, bad—in every situation, they say the word ‘Ram’. Once a devotee came to Lord Buddha and asked, “Suppose there is no god then I am wasting my whole time doing ‘Ram Ram Ram’?”

This seems to be a very simple question to us because we ignore the time, energy and effort a true devotee gives. This type of doubts will come if you invest your whole life in god, but if you invest just 10 minutes a week then you will not get this doubt. But if you invest your whole life in god then the doubt will obviously arise: “Am I wasting time doing this?”

Gautama Buddha replied, "No." The devotee felt great relief. Whenever disciples of Buddha asked such questions on the existence of god, he used to remain silent but this was the first time he had answered 'no God'. The struggle between god and no god came to an end finally; the message spread across town. Just imagine the freedom, no god meant nobody sitting up there keeping an account of what you did and what you did not do, to punish you when you are in hell or heaven. So, throughout the day, celebrations happened. In the evening, during the gathering, another man came and asked the same question, to which Buddha replied: "Yes God."

What Buddha was trying to convey is that if you believe there is God or if you believe there is no God, both are in the same boat. I believe this, you believe that; you can believe whatever you want. Everybody can believe whatever they want, it need not have anything to do with reality as such. There are people who do bad karma and simultaneously believe in god; there also exist people who do righteous karma but do not believe in god. What matters is 'karma'.

Rajneesh Osho was a master of controversies because one way was never the same as the other. Every human being comes from different regions, having different experiences and thought processes. Everyone cannot think in the same direction. Thus, he explored his own way of life, expanded his own path of success. This is something that a thinking mind, a logical mind, a creative mind, could understand things in a certain way in a different perspective. This is because there is no right or wrong in doing things in certain ways.

There are 110 ways to achieve salvation in Vigyan Bhairav tantra. Like a mathematics problem can be solved with numerous processes with many different methods, but the final answer will be the same. Same with spiritual practices. There are numerous methods to achieve a higher level of consciousness. The question is: has it worked for an individual or not? If it has worked for an individual to evolve into a higher state of being, it doesn't matter whether it is right or wrong, whether others agree or not, it simply doesn't matter.

1.2 Manifestation of God and Energy

Since ancient times, people have argued over and discussed the idea of God and energy. Throughout history, it has served as a source of motivation, solace and hope for numerous people. An approach to comprehend the relationship between the divine and the material world is through the manifestation of God and energy. Energy flowing through all living things and the belief that everything in the universe is interconnected have become widely accepted concepts in recent years. We shall discuss how to comprehend and use the manifestation of energy and God in our daily lives in this essay.

God's Manifestation

For thousands of years, numerous religions and spiritual practices have included the idea of God's appearance. It alludes to the notion that God can manifest himself in various ways or incarnations in order to converse with and lead humanity. The term 'avatars' in Hinduism, for instance, alludes to Lord Vishnu's many earthly incarnations, who came to balance good and evil.

According to Christianity, God appears in the teachings and deeds of Jesus Christ. It is thought that God took on human form in the person of Jesus in order to deliver humanity from sin and provide a way to eternal life. Similar to this, Islam views the teachings of Prophet Muhammad—who was regarded as God's last messenger—as the manifestation of God.

God's manifestation can be seen in non-religious settings as well. For some, it can be seen in nature, the wonder and amazement it evokes, as well as the beauty and intricacy of the world around us. Others can see it in deeds of love and compassion that they attribute to an unseen force.

Many people might find solace and inspiration in the ways that God manifests himself. It gives life a feeling of direction and significance and the conviction that a greater power is directing and assisting us on our journey.

Manifestation of Energy

The concept of energy is another way to understand the connection between the physical world and the divine. Energy refers to the force that powers all living things and is present in all aspects of the universe. It is believed that energy can be harnessed and directed to achieve specific goals, such as healing or spiritual growth.

The idea of energy as a force that can be manipulated and directed is present in many spiritual practices, such as Reiki and Qi Gong. In these practices, energy is believed to flow through the body and can be directed to specific areas to promote healing and balance.

Energy is also present in daily interactions with individuals and the environment around us. Times of happiness, love and thankfulness provide positive energy, whereas times of rage, fear and melancholy produce negative energy.

Relationship Between God and Energy

Despite their apparent differences, energy and the manifestation of God are closely related. According to popular belief, energy originates from God and permeates the entirety of the cosmos. The presence of energy in every facet of creation, from the tiniest particles to the grandest galaxies, provides evidence for this relationship.

The fact that energy may be focused and utilised for particular goals, like healing or spiritual development, can also be understood as a connection between God and energy. According to popular belief, we can communicate with the divine and gain access to higher states of awareness by drawing energy from the universe.

Depending on one's religious or spiritual views, there are various ways to comprehend the manifestation of God and energy. Some may view it as the work of a superior force that is directing and aiding us on our trip. Others could perceive it as a natural power that can be controlled and directed towards particular goals.

Omnipresence Nature of God

The idea of God's omnipresence has been argued and pondered over for many years. It serves as a key tenet of numerous religious traditions and is frequently used to characterise the character of the divine. The concept of omnipresence simply refers to God being everywhere at all times. For many believers, this idea is a source of solace and direction, but it is also a cause of debate for those who do not believe in a greater power.

Ancient religious writings like the Bible, Quran and Bhagavad Gita all contain references to omnipresence. The omnipresence of God is mentioned multiple times in the Bible. "Where can I go from your Spirit?"—for instance, asks Psalm 139:7-10. "Where can I run to escape you? You are there regardless of where I make my bed—in the depths or the sky. Even there, if I ascend on the wings of the morning or land on the opposite side of the sea, your hand will hold me firmly and lead the way."

Similar to this, Allah is said to be everywhere in the Quran. In verse 57 of Surah Al-Hadid, it is written, "He is with you wherever you are." In several sections of the Bhagavad Gita, God's omnipresence is also discussed. For instance, Lord Krishna declares in Chapter 9, Verse 4, "By Me, in My unmanifest form, this entire universe is penetrated. Though I am not in them, all beings are in Me."

Even though the idea of omnipresence is widely accepted, some people still disagree with it. Some contend that the notion of God's omnipresence is only a divine personification of human needs and desires. Others contend that because the idea of omnipresence implies that God is both inside and outside of creation, it is fundamentally contradictory.

One way to comprehend the idea of omnipresence is to think about what God is like. God is typically described as limitless, eternal and transcendent in religious traditions. This implies that God exists outside of space, time and the physical universe. But God is also immanent, which means that God is present in the world. The idea of omnipresence reflects the paradoxical character of God.

Thinking on the connection between God and creation can help us comprehend the idea of omnipresence. God is revered as the universe's designer in a wide variety of religious traditions. This proves that God is involved in every facet of creation. God, however, is distinct from creation because He is not constrained by the universal physical laws. God is able to be present everywhere and at all times because of this division.

Believers frequently find solace and direction in the idea of omnipresence. People who believe in God may experience a sense of belonging to something greater than themselves. Knowing that God is constantly keeping an eye on them can also give one a sense of security.

आदित्यानामहं विष्णुर्ज्योतिषां रविरंशुमान् |
मरीचिर्मरुतामस्मि नक्षत्राणामहं शशी || 21||

Bhagavad Gita, Vibhuti Yog, 10.21

I am Vishnu. Amongst twelve sons of Aditi; I am sun amongst luminous objects. Know Me to be Marichi amongst the maruts, and the moon amongst the stars in the night sky.

वेदानां सामवेदोऽस्मि देवानामस्मि वासवः |
इन्द्रियाणां मनश्चास्मि भूतानामस्मि चेतना || 22||

Bhagavad Gita, Vibhuti Yog, 10.22

Amongst the Vedas I am the Samaveda, and Indra amongst the celestial gods. I am the mind amongst the senses; amongst the living beings I am consciousness.

रुद्राणां शङ्करश्चास्मि वित्तेशो यक्षरक्षसाम् |
वसूनां पावकश्चास्मि मेरुः शिखरिणामहम् || 23||

I am Sankar amongst the Rudras; I am Kuber amongst the semi-celestial beings and demons. I am Agni amongst the vasus and Meru amongst the mountains.

अश्वत्थः सर्ववृक्षाणां देवर्षीणां च नारदः |
गन्धर्वाणां चित्ररथः सिद्धानां कपिलो मुनिः || 26||

Bhagavad Gita, Vibhuti Yog, 10.26

Amongst trees I am the sacred peepal tree; amongst the celestial sages

I am Narad. Amongst the Gandharvas I am Chitrath, and amongst the siddhas I am sage Kapil.

उच्चै:श्रवसमश्वानां विद्धि माममृतोद्भवम् |
ऐरावतं गजेन्द्राणां नराणां च नराधिपम् || 27||

Amongst horses know Me to be Ucchaihshrava, begotten from the churning of the ocean of nectar. I am Airavata amongst all lordly elephants, and the king amongst humans.

अनन्तश्चास्मि नागानां वरुणो यादसामहम् |
पितृणामर्यमा चास्मि यम: संयमतामहम् || 29||

Amongst the snakes I am Anant; amongst aquatics I am Varun. Amongst the departed ancestors I am Aryama; amongst dispensers of law I am Yamraj, the lord of death.

प्रह्लादश्चास्मि दैत्यानां काल: कलयतामहम् |
मृगाणां च मृगेन्द्रोऽहं वैनतेयश्च पक्षिणाम् || 30||

Amongst demons I am Prahlad; amongst all that controls I am time. Know me to be the lion amongst animals, and Garud amongst the birds.

The subtle energy, which is the atom in its complex form, is the fundamental basis of all elements that exist in this universe.

Whatever we see or feel in nature, everything is made up of energy. Every material object is made of energy which forms atoms in the collective form. Consider a table, chair, board, pen, paper, iron, steel, plastic… everything in this universe we observe so far is made of energy. The difference between two objects is due to the arrangement and structural setup of energy levels at the subatomic level.

Thus, it can be said that everything in this universe is a manifestation of god Krishna, which is a tremendous divine energy in its subtle form.

Cosmic Sounds

The universe is a phenomenon that is both audible and visual. In many historical societies, sound has played a significant role in spirituality as it is a fundamental component of the cosmos. Sound has been utilised to communicate with the divine and transcend the physical world for thousands of years, from the prehistoric Vedic hymns to the Gregorian chants of Christianity, from the Australian Aboriginal song lines to the Om chant of Hinduism. The connection between sound and spirituality will be discussed in this essay, as well as the methods in which cosmic sounds have been employed to bring about spiritual awareness.

For thousands of years, sound has been a significant component of spirituality. Sound is employed in many religions to transcend the physical realm and establish a connection with the divine. The Om mantra is used in Hinduism to induce meditation and facilitate communication with the divine. Chanting is a technique used in Buddhism to concentrate the mind and reach a state of serenity and clarity. Five times a day, the call to prayer is recited in Islam to remind believers of their relationship with God.

Organised religions are not the only ones to use music in spirituality. In many indigenous cultures, ancestors are honoured and a connection to the spirit realm is made via song and dance. Aboriginal people in Australia utilise song lines to find their way around and stay connected to the land. Arctic Inuit utilise throat singing to conjure up trance-like states and connect with spirits.

There are countless sounds across the cosmos that are inaudible to humans. Scientists have spent decades researching these cosmic sounds, such as electromagnetic waves and gravitational waves. However, only recently have researchers looked into their spiritual implications.

The cosmic microwave background radiation (CMB) is one of the most well-known examples of cosmological noise. The oldest light in the cosmos is this radiation, which is a by-product of the Big Bang. Arno Penzias and Robert Wilson made the initial discovery in 1965, for which they were given the Nobel Prize in Physics in 1978.

The CMB is frequently described as the 'sound of the universe', because it captures the state of the universe barely 380,000 years after the Big Bang. It has a frequency of roughly 160.2 GHz and is a very faint hiss that can be heard in all directions. Cosmologists have examined the CMB in great detail and it has given them valuable information about the early cosmos.

The CMB has additionally been investigated spiritually. Some people think that the CMB holds knowledge of the divine and the nature of the cosmos. They think that the CMB can be used to reach spiritual enlightenment since it is a manifestation of the sound of creation.

The sound of the sun is another cosmic sound that has been investigated spiritually. The sun emits a variety of sounds, including acoustic, electromagnetic and plasma waves. Instruments like the Michelson Doppler Imager (MDI) on the Solar and Heliospheric Observatory (SOHO) satellite can pick up these noises.

Spiritual practices have long employed the sounds of the sun. Hinduism considers the sun to be a divinity, and its noises are thought to have healing powers. The sun was revered in ancient Egypt as Ra, and people there thought that its tones had healing and benevolent properties.

Additionally, each planet in our solar system emits a distinctive sound. The magnetic field of the planet and the charged particles in its atmosphere interact to produce these noises. They frequently go by the name ‘choruses’, since they sound like a choir.

Sounds and vibrations have a deep impact on each and every particle in this universe. The impression of sound has a deep impact on human thoughts and emotions. When someone is happy then he likes to listen to some kind of music; if someone is sad, they like to listen to a different kind of music; for love there is music and for suspense, there is another kind. Each and every music has sounds of a different range and vibration that we scientifically call as pitch and amplitude. Now, suppose we didn’t have a tongue, we can only utter Aa, Uu, Mm. Without a tongue, we cannot speak a single word or utter any single other sound. Therefore, these three sounds are considered the basic and universal of all sounds and vibrations. If we utter this sound together—AUM.

1.3 Nature of God (Brahma, Vishnu and Mahesh)

Brahma (The Creator)

One of Hinduism's most revered gods, Brahma is regarded as the universe's creator. He was created from a lotus that came from Lord Vishnu, the universe's protector, according to Hindu mythology. The four Vedas and the four directions are represented by Brahma's four heads and four limbs in popular art.

The universe came into existence because Brahma, the creator, created it. Compared to some of the other Hindu deities, including Vishnu and Shiva, Brahma is not as commonly revered. This is partially due to the fact that he is regarded as a creator god and plays a less significant function in maintaining the universe than Vishnu or Shiva do. But Brahma is still recognised as a significant entity.

Thus, every creation must have a creator and without a creator, no creation could exist. This whole world is not a by-product of random events. It is well organised and governed by laws of nature. The creative energy is 'Brahma'.

Vishnu (The Preserver)

He is the preserver, the divine source of energy that maintains the universe. Let's try to understand with an example: when you talk to a new person, you get close and become friends easily. When you tell something which hurts your friend, however close the friendship is doesn't matter, it will collapse. The most complex and important thing is to maintain the creation. Whether it is a relationship, a baby, a new home or any substance, perseverance is the most difficult task in the process of creation.

The most divine form of Vishnu is Krishna, the god of love. Let us understand who Krishna is in actual form.

Krishna is the one who possesses the power to behead anyone at the first abuse but also tolerates millions of abuses every second in this Kaliyuga—he is Krishna. One who has a powerful destructive weapon like the Sudarshan Chakra but also steals everyone's hearts with the madhur sound of a flute—he is Krishna. One who has a vast golden kingdom like Dwarka but also grazes with cattle and goats in arid grasslands—he is Krishna. One who has all the devis and devas at his feet waiting for his command but also has best friends like Sudama who do not have anything except Krishna.

During the furious war of Kurukshetra, amid the roaring sounds of arrows, artillery, trumpets, drums, cymbals and bagpipes, it was difficult for Krishna to get Arjuna to take direction and control of the chariot. Krishna instructs Arjuna that if Arjuna needs to take the chariot right, to kick Krishna's left shoulder; if he needs to take the chariot left, to kick his left shoulder. If he needs to stop the chariot, to kick the middle of his shoulders; if he needs to speed up the chariot, to kick his shoulders twice. This is the humility of Krishna. One who serves his clients even after getting pain, he is Krishna.

The most significant character or avatar of Lord Vishnu is Krishna, whose essence is true love. No human being will become 100% the way we want them to be and this is the bitter truth that all humans in this world will disappoint us in the end. Not because they will do some wrong but nobody can fulfil all the unrealistic expectations we have for them.

You say that you love rain, but you open your umbrella when it rains.

You say that you love the sun, but you find a shaded spot when the sun shines.

You say that you love the wind, but you close your windows when the wind blows.

This is why I am afraid, you say that you love me too.

William Shakespeare

Today, true love doesn't exist. Love is beyond talks and emotions. Love requires a great sense of integrity and commitment. That emotion is not love in which there are expectations because they are like bondage. You bind their hands with your unlimited expectations, and you think it's love? Love gives freedom, not bondage. Today, everyone has some or the other expectations to get benefits in return. Either family members, friends, guardians or any other, everyone wants to fulfil their unfulfilled expectations from whom they love the most.

There is a thin layer between love—prem—and lust, that is 'moh'. Love boosts courage but lust makes a coward. Love comes from compassion but lust comes from pride. Love gives freedom but lust gives bondage. Love gives peace but lust gives suffering; love gives knowledge but lust gives ignorance. Love wills one to sacrifice but lust wills one to hold and retain. Love is righteousness, the divine dharma, and lust is adharma. In a practical sense where there is love, there doesn't exist lust.

Krishna is not just an emblem to own for devotion. There is no copyright issued on god and devotion. No one could own Krishna then, no one can own him now and in the present Kaliyuga, it is even impossible to own him. God is not to own for one's self because god is only a source of joy and peace for everyone in this world full of sorrow. This is how we must see Krishna. He is not a complex man but just a simple joyful human being.

In any given situation, be it in love or in war, he remains joyful. Even in the battlefield of Kurukshetra, he was cracking jokes—that says a lot about him. Krishna lived a joyful life even in a situation where he was separated from his mother Devaki soon after birth, separated from Yashoda who nurtured him, couldn't marry Radha whom he loved the most, his vast army got vanquished in the Mahabharata war, his sons killed themselves in a fight due to a curse, his golden kingdom Dwarka got seized in the ocean. Still, he was sitting in the shade of a tree in the middle of a forest, playing the flute with love and affection, with animals and birds enjoying and dancing around him with joy and happiness, like nothing had happened at all!

Shiva (The Destroyer)

When a subject is created, it will be destroyed one day. Nothing in this universe is permanent. This creation is also temporary, an illusion to the eye of humans. When human beings raise their consciousness, they can get the knowledge of truth. The veil of ignorance will be removed and the light of knowledge will enlighten their life.

The whole universe and cosmos is filled with vacuum, that is, nothingness. Only a very little space of the entire cosmos has stars, planets, galaxies, matter and so on but the rest of the universe is empty. No light wave, no matter, no particle, no sound frequency. A very large proportion of the universe has nothing and remains undisturbed; therefore, nothingness is more in this universe than somethingness. That's the nature of Shiva—nothingness. Shiva is the non-physical dimension of existence.

The nature of Shiva encourages us to live in a higher consciousness, sacrificing our material and bodily success because neither beauty nor money in life is permanent. The most beautiful person today will definitely become old one day. A person who is very rich once may not remain rich like that. Stock markets and businesses always witness ups and downs. So, nothing is permanent in life. What is permanent, Shiva says, is knowledge. Nobody can steal, nobody can burn, and nobody can bury knowledge. The more we spread knowledge, the wealthier we will become.

Chapter 2

BIOPHYSICS ANALYSIS

Yog Shastra

For millennia, people have been interested in and studying Kundalini yoga, which aims to awaken the dormant spiritual energy at the base of the spine. Understanding the physiological and biophysical principles underlying this age-old practice has garnered increasing interest in recent years.

In order to understand the mysteries of this ancient practise, biophysics analysis of Kundalini in Yog Shastra aims to investigate the physical, chemical, and biological elements of Kundalini yoga. In addition to shedding new light on the intricate interactions between mind, body, and spirit in Kundalini yoga practice, this multidisciplinary method strives to close the knowledge gap between contemporary science and conventional wisdom.

In this chapter, we'll go more deeply into the Yog Shastra's biophysics explanation of Kundalini and consider how it might affect how we think about consciousness and the human condition.

2.1 Existence of Spirits and Souls

Philosophical and religious debates about the existence of spirits and souls date back many millennia. While some people hold the notion that spirits and souls exist, others contend that there is no empirical data to back up these claims.

The Significance of Spirits and Souls Historically and Culturally

For thousands of years, human culture and religion have incorporated the idea of spirits and souls. The creation and destruction of the natural world were ascribed to them, which were assumed to exist in prehistoric cultures. For instance, the Greeks held that there was a hierarchy of gods and goddesses, each with its own attributes and duties. Romans also held a belief in ghosts and souls, which they referred to as geniuses and larvas.

This concept is still prevalent in many indigenous societies. For instance, many Native American tribes hold that spirits and souls—which they refer to as the Great Spirit—are real and that these beings are in charge of preserving the harmony of nature.

The idea of the soul is central to the religious doctrines of the Abrahamic religions. These faiths hold that God endowed people with souls, which are the non-physical parts of the human body that house a person's individuality and essence. It is believed that the soul is immortal and will go on after the body has passed away.

The existence of spirits and souls is supported by science in the following ways:

Despite the fact that the existence of spirits and souls cannot be proven through scientific means, certain researchers have made an effort to do so. Professor of psychology, medicine, neurology, psychiatry, and surgery at the University of Arizona, Dr Gary Schwartz is one such researcher.

Dr Schwartz has tested the presence of the soul in a number of ways. In one study, he asked patients who were at the end of their lives to choose a photo of a loved one from a collection of random images while their brain activity was being tracked. The findings demonstrated that the patients' brain activity differed noticeably from that of the control group when they recognised the image of a loved one. According to Dr Schwartz, this experiment supports the existence of the soul, which he holds to be the source of all of our emotions and feelings.

Dr Ian Stevenson, a different scholar, has done substantial research on the theory of reincarnation, which is connected to the concept of the soul. Dr Stevenson has researched instances in which young children have memories of former lifetimes and are able to convey information about those lives that they would not have been able to learn through conventional ways. Despite criticism, others contend that his research supports the presence of the soul and the possibility of reincarnation.

Objections Against the Notion of Spirits and Souls

Some contend that there is proof for the existence of spirits and souls, while others counter that there is no concrete evidence to back up these claims. The lack of empirical proof is one argument against their existence. While some scientists have made an effort to demonstrate the soul's existence, their tests have come under fire for their approach and lack of scientific rigour.

The claim that spirits and souls are not required to explain human behaviour and emotions is another denial of their existence. Many contend that our emotions and sensations may be described by brain activity and chemical interactions, despite the fact that the idea of the soul is employed to do so. When we talk about energy, there exists different forms of energy of different values. Heat, wind, cold, electricity, even a moving object possess potential and kinetic energy.

Biophysics states that in a human body, there exists different energy like chemical energy at cellular level known as enzymes, emotional energy known as hormones, physical energy known as minerals and proteins, mental energy or brain cells metabolism, spiritual energy or subtle energy.

Understanding Yog Philosophy of Ancient India

The life energy called 'prana', which means soul, has its own significance role in the regulation of the living body. Biological life energy in ancient India is divided into 5 forms that exists within our body.

- Prana vayu in chest and head that governs inspiration, propulsion, forward momentum.
- Apana Vayu in pelvis that regulates elimination, downward and outward movement.
- Samana vayu in navel that regulates assimilation, inner absorption and consolidation.
- Udana vayu in throat regulates growth, speech, expression, upward movement.
- Vyana vayu in whole body that regulates blood circulation and expansiveness (ability to expand).

There is a detailed process and instructions to command and control these energies in Yog Shastra to have a healthy and disease-free life. Extreme command over the life energy gives supernatural powers, which are called 'siddhis'. These energies lie within our body in supressed form due to our modern day-to-day lifestyle. By following yog sidhanta, one can awaken these energies.

Understanding Law of Thermodynamics and Conservation of Energy

'Energy can neither be created nor be destroyed', so considering the fact that if one cannot utilise or awaken the life energy within the body to get that energy to manifest or utilise it to receive some benefits in one's lifetime, after death of this physical human body, the subtle energy gets released into the environment and is converted into some form of energy which we call 'paranormal or ghost energy'.

This energy has a significant existence in nature. It wanders or deviates in nature for some 10-13 days and then converts into another form, which might be a by-product of another living creature. That's why in India, a ritual is followed for 12 days to give peace to the soul of deceased. From 'kriya', firing the dead body to release the soul to 'sraddha' puja, a ceremonial ritual for the soul of deceased to get peace.

नैनम चिंदंति शास्त्राणि नैनम देहाति पावकाः

न चैनम् केलदयंत्यपापो ना शोषयति मारुताः

Bhagavad Gita 2:23

Weapons cannot shred the soul, nor can fire burn it. Water cannot wet it, nor can the wind dry it.

2.2 How It Feels to Experience God and Energy

Everything we observe and experience is energy of different levels. When we turn on a fan, the electric energy gets converted into wind energy. As in a heater, electric energy gets converted into heat energy. In a washing machine, electric energy is converted into kinetic energy. So, whatever home appliance we use in our home for our comfort is energy at a minimal level, which can be considered as smaller than a drop of water within the ocean.

When we feel hot, we use the AC to withdraw cool wind energy. Just think that it's summer and 45 degrees outside and you don't even have a fan; it will be a disaster. Imagine when you are in a desert, very thirsty and after two days of long journey, you see an oasis in front of you, how would you feel?

Thus, when you get the right thing at the right time, it becomes a blessing; even the water would seem like nectar. This is what it means to experience Krishna in real life.

समोऽहं सर्वभूतेषु न मे द्वेष्योऽस्ति न प्रिय: |
ये भजन्ति तु मां भक्त्या मयि ते तेषु चाप्यहम् || 29||

Bhagavad Gita Chapter 9:29

In this shloka, Krishna says that, "Love is the only divine expression in this universe, it is natural in all living creatures. The only way to conquer this whole world is love. Even a devotee can conquer me and I am glad to be conquered through true and unconditional love."

Love wins all, love yourself and others, because love is the only weapon to conquer the whole world in just a minute. It may take years and years of war to conquer a country, years and years to convince people and years to get economic power but if one lives in pure Krishna consciousness, loves all living creatures, he will definitely conquer the hearts of all, enemies as well.

Siddhas, yogis, rishis forget themselves in the love of Krishna. For example, if someone explains how it feels to get a glass of water when they are thirsty in a dry desert, you can get an overview but you will not understand anything till you haven't experienced it.

The same with Krishna. However nicely someone might describe the experience, you will not understand anything till you haven't experienced Krishna in your real life. This is the joy of salvation and cannot be described in words.

2.3 How to Experience God and Energy

Kundalini and siddhi. This is a question for which sages and rishis spent years and years to get the answer.

Humans cannot see colours beyond a certain range of wavelength or listen to sounds beyond a certain range of Hertz. The god Krishna exists beyond this. A common human cannot experience Krishna without any spiritual effort. To experience this energy of higher consciousness, one needs to be ready and spiritually strong to resist the energy of Krishna.

There are many spiritual ways in 'bigyan bhairav tantra' that raise your consciousness, spiritually called 'Kundalini' in absolute rapid form, which is risky and not advisable and on the other hand, there also spiritual ways to raise 'Kundalini' organically, which is advisable and recommended.

According to yoga philosophy, Kundalini is a subtle energy that lies suppressed within the human body. If one tries to awaken Kundalini, he experiences super powers 'siddhis' and when this biological body termed as 'Shiva' meets with Kundalini energy termed 'Shakti', the doors of salvation or moksha unlocks for that individual.

You may have seen many yogis and rishis act like they are mad. It's not that they are born mad but due to some spiritual practice, they raise Kundalini in such rapid form and experience Krishna that it's impossible for a biological body to resist such higher energy. It's like transferring 2000V of electric current in a wire which has potential to resist only 20V of electric current. The wire will melt and fuse. The same stands for a human body to experience Krishna.

Kundalini and Sex Energy

Our ancient texts are written in Sanskrit and in the contemporary world, only a handful of people know Sanskrit. Our ancient texts were translated in different languages by many scholars but the main foundational facts were manipulated and interpreted in accordance with western culture. In present times, sex is considered weird, not to be talked about in public, even sometimes equated with disrespect when it comes to gynaecologists.

Nothing in this creation exists uselessly. Every element in this creation has its own essence and is essential for the existence and sustenance of the human race. We are talking about life energy. In ancient times, all the architecture of temples depicted the nature and importance of 'Kama Sutras'; it was not considered a taboo.

In those days, people understood the life process that was essential to sustain the human race on this earth. Many scholars and translators' portrayed sex and spirituality as different and opposite to one another but in the true sense, it's not. The life energy that gives 'Kama basna', desire for sex is to be manifested into spiritual energy, which we call 'Kundalini' and it can have the most dangerous side effects if not handled and regulated properly because it has the potential to change the nature and self of an individual.

According to Patanjali yog sutras, there are seven chakras in the human body. In all human beings, at the initial phase of life, energy lies in root chakra or 'muladhara chakra', which is a power point located at sex organs. The nature of this root power point or muladhara chakra is to create an urge and desire for sex, which is important for creation of a new individual and responsible for the existence of human race.

This energy can create new individuals through reproduction and that's why it is the most potential creative energy within the human body. This energy accumulated in muladhara chakra or sex organ is unable to find a way to flow due to which an individual is forced by its nature to masturbate and release the energy. But this life energy can be raised from the bottom chakra to upper chakras with some spiritual practices and yoga tantra sadhana.

The life energy at different power points or chakras regulates the nature of consciousness of an individual. The life energy remains constant but it's the nature of consciousness regulated by Kundalini that creates the urge. When Kundalini is at muladhara, there comes an urge for material and bodily pleasures, in swadhisthana-creativity, manipura-will power, anahata-love and compassion, visuddha-communication, ajna-awareness, intuition and perception, sahasrara-moksha or wisdom.

Sex energy and spirituality are just two faces of the same coin. Life energy ignites an urge for pleasure, satisfaction and desire, which is constant for both sex and spirituality but the difference is in sex, it's all about material and body and spirituality is all about God, self-realisation and knowledge. Both the natures of energy are important for human existence. It's like a boat, where you cross the river or you cross the pond or canal, the boat remains the same.

There is a detailed guided process to manifest life energy from the bottom chakras to upper chakras in ancient texts. It's a very simple but difficult process of self-realisation, which, if not done properly, can backfire and have devastating effects on life.

God Within Us

A fundamental element of Indian religious and spiritual teachings is the notion that God is present within every one of us. This idea stems from the conviction that God is omnipresent and that everyone has the capacity to become divine.

The Hindu term for the idea of God existing within us is Atma, which is frequently translated as the soul. It is thought that the Atma is a person's true nature and that it is identical to Brahman, the supreme reality. One of the most significant Hindu books, the Bhagavad Gita, asserts that every living thing possesses an Atma, which is an everlasting and unchanging being unaffected by birth, death, or any other changes of the material world.

The deepest self, which is distinct from the physical body and the mind, is referred to as the Atma. The Gita asserts that the Atma is the origin of all knowledge and that the purpose of human life is to reach this knowledge.

Ancient Hindu texts known as the Upanishads place a strong emphasis on the Atma. The Atma is the ultimate reality that lies at the foundation of all creation, and that it is the cause of all existence. Pure consciousness, which transcends the boundaries of the body and mind, is what is meant when we refer to the Atma. The Upanishads also advise practising meditation and other spiritual disciplines in order to realise one's Atma, which they say is the ultimate aim of life.

Buddha-nature, the inherent capacity for enlightenment present in all sentient beings, is the Buddhist term for the idea that God is inside us. All living things have the capacity to achieve Buddhahood, which is the ultimate enlightenment. The essence of a person, which transcends the bounds of the body and the mind, is referred to as having a Buddha-nature. It is regarded as the most fundamental and pure component of a person's being.

The Buddha-nature is said to exist in all beings, according to the Mahayana school of Buddhism, and it serves as the basis for all Buddhist practices. The realisation of the Buddha-nature, according to the Mahayana literature, is the ultimate aim of Buddhist practice and can be accomplished by developing wisdom and compassion. One of the most significant Mahayana texts, the Lotus Sutra, asserts that everyone has the capacity to become a Buddha and that this capacity is innate in their Buddha-nature.

The idea of God existing within us is known as the soul, or Jiva, in Jainism. According to Jainism, every living thing possesses an immortal soul that never changes. The innermost self, as distinguished from the physical body and the mind, is referred to as the soul. The soul is the origin of consciousness and is in charge of controlling both the body and the mind. The ultimate purpose of human life is the realisation of the soul, which can be accomplished by spiritual exercises like meditation and self-control.

The idea of God existing inside us is known as the Divine Spark, or Jot, in Sikhism. According to Sikhism, each person possesses a Divine

Spark that is the same as God. The innermost self, which is distinct from the physical body and the consciousness, is referred to as the Divine Spark. The ultimate objective of human life is the realisation of the Divine Spark, which can be accomplished through spiritual exercises like meditation and selfless service.

सुहृन्मित्रार्युदासीनमध्यस्थद्वेष्यबन्धुषु |
साधुष्वपि च पापेषु समबुद्धिर्विशिष्यते || 9||

Bhagavad Gita 6:9

"The yogis look upon all—well-wishers, friends, foes, the pious, and the sinners—with an impartial intellect. The yogi, who is of equal intellect towards friend, companion, and foe, neutral among enemies and relatives, and unbiased between the righteous and sinful, is considered to be distinguished among humans."

अहमात्मा गुडाकेश सर्वभूताशयस्थित: |
अहमादिश्च मध्यं च भूतानामन्त एव च || 20||

Bhagavad Gita 10:20

"O Arjun, I am seated in the heart of all living entities. I am the beginning, middle, and end of all beings."

The Kundalini life energy is the most creative energy that lies in subtle form within us. We came into existence within this creation. The vast ultimate energy that exists or flows in this world also exists and flows within us. We don't know how to use this energy, that's a different thing but we have that most potent energy within us that people call 'GOD' in English terms.

Every day in the morning, if we start the day with this thought in our mind, that today wherever we step, we will create a peaceful, joyful world. If we fall down and fail hundreds of times in a day, then it simply doesn't matter. For a committed karma yogi, there is no such thing called failure.

If one falls down and fails 100 times, a hundred lessons are waiting for you to learn. If one is committed like this to create what we really care for, our mind gets organised and once our mind gets organised, the way we think becomes the way we feel. Our emotions get organised and all the energy within our body also gets organised to actually fulfil what we want.

Once your thoughts, emotions and energies are organised, our body will get organised. And this is when our physical existence 'Shiva' meet our mental existence 'Shakti' within us. At this moment, our ability to create and manifest what we want becomes phenomenal. Thus, we are the creator in some ways. The source of creation is functioning within us every moment of our life.

God and Imagination

Whatever we imagine about God, a personified intelligent being comes to our mind as we see in calendars and television serials. First of all, we need to understand that God is an entity from a different dimension. We need to change our perspective of seeing things if we want to understand a thing from a different dimension, which is a completely new thing to us.

God is not limited to some kind of certain body shape or size. There is no single manifestation of god. God is not limited to our thoughts and emotions. If we want to understand God, then first of all, we need to prepare ourselves to understand God.

From many experiences of yogis and siddhas, we can guess that it takes some average 3 to 4 years to reach a certain level of yoga and consciousness. Though the time period varies from one individual to another according to their consciousness and concentration, it takes a lot of determination.

According to Patanjali yog sutras, there are a total 8 systematic processes or steps of yoga to be followed. Yam, niyam, asan, pranayam, pratyahara, dharna, dhyan, samadhi. Today, in most government and private schools and colleges, students don't attend class, which is a breach of the 1st step of yoga itself as a child i.e. yama (self-discipline), and also neither students nor adults follow code of conduct of any institutions, which is again a breach of the second rule, niyama-2nd step of yoga.

It's a clear cut prescription that it may be fatal if yoga is practised in a wrong way without supervision of a guru because yoga is a most potential process. And the most potent things are always the most dangerous.

But today, most yoga and religious centres just make people do something for money and business. Today, spirituality becomes a business but then it will be a great and divine act if the money earned through such business is used for the good of mankind and human security. But there are many fake sadhus and sanyasis who preach rubbish and even engage in criminal activities like rape and murder. This is how the essence of spirituality is destroyed. Today, Indian culture and philosophy have become just a formality in the world.

Chapter 3

DIVINE RULES OF NATURE

Analysis on Laws of Thermodynamics and Energy Conservation

Analysing Satapatha Brahmana (Yajur Veda) and manusmriti, we can clearly get the depiction of the first avatar of Lord Vishnu on earth as 'Matshya' avatara. It means fish and if we study modern scientific reports on the environment, the scientists have concluded that life originates from water.

The first form of complex living creature evolved in aquatic and marine spheres. The effect of Navagraha according to astrology is experienced consciously or unconsciously by everyone. Modern scientists have discovered that all planets in our solar system have direct influence over Earth.

Sun for light and ultimate energy, moon for tides, Jupiter attracts asteroids to keep them away from the Earth and so on. Our historical texts are the primary source of information on creation.

3.1 Creation of Universe

Human Perception on Creation

Illusion is a concept that is ingrained in the human psyche. We've all been duped by something we believed to be true only to discover that it was only an illusion. This could be as straightforward as a magic trick or as sophisticated as an illusion that causes someone to think they are experiencing something that they are not.

A mistaken view of reality is described by the definition of the word 'illusion' itself. It may also be used to describe a deceptive appearance or impression that is not consistent with the reality. The term has historically been used to denote many types of deception in literature, philosophy, psychology, and even religion.

Ancient Greek philosophy has one of the earliest mentions of the idea of illusion. The great Greek thinker Plato wrote in great detail about the nature of reality and the delusion that can skew our perception of it. In his well-known allegory of the cave, Plato describes a group of prisoners who are chained up and positioned against a wall in a pitch-black cave.

A fire is raging behind the inmates, and people are walking by, carrying objects between the flames and the prisoners. In front of the convicts, the shadows of these things are projected onto the wall, where they are taken for reality.

Plato utilises this fable to convey the idea that the delusions we conjure up in our imaginations can skew how we perceive the world. He thought that only by escaping these delusions and seeing things as they really were, could true knowledge and insight be attained.

Other philosophers throughout history have repeated this thought, including Descartes, who is known for saying, "I think, therefore I am." This phrase implies that although our perceptions and ideas may be delusions, the fact that we are thinking creatures is evidence that we do, in fact, exist.

A common literary theme is illusion, especially in works of science fiction and fantasy. The idea of illusion has been employed by authors to examine themes of power, control, and freedom, including JRR Tolkien and George Orwell.

Sauron, a fictional figure from Tolkien's 'Lord of the Rings', utilises a magical ring to conjure up illusions and manipulate people around him. To destroy the ring and save Middle Earth, the main character, Frodo, must cross a world of illusion and deception.

Psychology has also looked into the concept of illusion, particularly when studying perception and cognition. Examples of illusions that show how our sense of reality can be altered by our brains include the Ames room illusion and the Müller-Lyer illusion. These deceptions demonstrate how our vision of reality can be easily manipulated and how our brains perceive visual stimuli based on context and prior experiences.

Illusion can also refer to the tricks of magicians and illusionists. Magic shows rely on the audience's belief in the illusion of what they are seeing. By creating a sense of wonder and disbelief, magicians are able to make the impossible seem possible.

However, the word 'illusion' can also have negative connotations. It can refer to a deception or falsehood that is intended to mislead or harm someone. In this sense, the word is often used to describe political propaganda or advertising that uses misleading tactics to persuade people.

In conclusion, the concept of illusion is complex and multifaceted.

Mother Nature-related human behaviour refers to how people interact with and behave in regard to the natural world. The sustainability of the earth and its inhabitants is directly impacted by this interaction, making it crucial. But lately, people have behaved mostly negatively towards Mother Nature, which has resulted in environmental degradation and all of its associated negative effects, including climate change, pollution, a loss of biodiversity, and natural disasters.

Humans have acted in ways that are harmful to Mother Nature in many different ways. These include overfishing, poaching, deforestation, pollution, and the use of non-renewable resources. Large areas of forest are cleared during deforestation to make way for urbanisation, agriculture, and logging. As a result, many species of animals and plants have lost their natural habitats and there has been a decline in biodiversity.

Through education and awareness, one of the most important ways to encourage good human behaviour towards Mother Nature is achieved. People must comprehend the value of a healthy environment and the effects of their behaviour on it. This can be done by implementing government regulations, educational initiatives, and public campaigns that support sustainable living.

है पृथिवी माता, सारे बिस्व मैं तुम जैसे ख्यमासील कोई नही। तुम्हारे धरती पर साधु बी रहते है और महा पापी बी क्रूर चरण तेरे सरीर पर रखके चलते है। कुछ लोग तेरे धरती पर पुण्य कर्म का फूल खिलते हैं और कुछ पाप् का लहू बी बहाते है, परंतु तुम सबको सहन करती हो। अपना सीना फाड़ कर सबको अन्न देती हो, सबका भरण पोषण करती हो। एक मा के भांति अपने सब अच्छे बुरे बच्चों का पालन पोषण करती हो। किसीका अहित नही करती हो। इसलिए मा तेरी ये मिट्टी इतनी पवित्र है, में इसे ही दैवित्य मानकर इसे ग्रहण करता हूँ।

Krishna in Mahabharata:

"O Mother Earth, there is no one as beautiful as you are in the whole world. Sadhus live on your land and great sinners also keep their cruel feet on your body. Some people bloom on your land for good deeds and some shed the blood of sin, but you tolerate them all. Tearing your chest, you give food to everyone, you feed everyone. You nurture all your good and bad children like a mother. You do not harm anyone. That's why this soil of yours is so sacred, I accept it, considering it as divine."

Human imagination is limited to a certain extent, which is not capable of understanding the vastness of God and energy. In a moment, we feel a certain thing is good and at the other moment, we feel the same thing to be bad. Every element in this universe is there for a reason. Let's understand this with a practical illustration.

Today, rain is considered bad as it hampers day-to-day life of millions of people. That's why there is a very famous saying in England, 'rain rain go away, come again another day'. In India, which is a tropical country, rain is always good for large diverse vegetation.

Realisation of Creation

God is the most finest, complete and independent in nature. So this question arises that 'if God is complete with its own, then why God created this universe or what was the necessity and requirement for the existence of this creation'?

We can feel the importance of certain things only in its absence in our times of need. When a certain thing is accumulated by us more than needed, no matter how expensive the thing is, it becomes unimportant and often, we ignore its value but on the other hand, no matter how cheap a thing is, if we don't get it in our time of need, then it feels like very expensive and we realise its value and importance.

Let's understand with some examples. A rich person who has accumulated much more wealth than needed, cannot realise the value of money but a poor person knows the value of every single penny. Value of water is not more than trash in coastal areas but the same drop of water turns into nectar in drought regions when there is no rain for a few years.

People ignore bread over burgers and pizza but during wars and revolts, unavailability of vegetables affects the staple diet of most people. We don't care about anyone in our lifetime but we feel the importance of that person only after his/her death. The one who always prays for happiness is the one who everyday suffers from sadness and trauma.

If there would be no emotion called sadness, then there would be happiness everywhere and in this situation, how could we realise the actual value of happiness? If there is no pain and suffering, how can we understand the value of relief? If there is no misery, then how can we realise the value of joy?

Thus, it's clear that we can realise the value of certain things only after we have realised both its presence and absence in our life. The same principle applies to our universe. Physical existence of this world is an illusion. No one is above God and energy because every living and non-living thing in this world is a manifested form of one stream of divine energy.

To get this divine knowledge of self-realisation, God created this world of illusion. This world of illusion prepares us to remove the veil of ignorance to make everyone realise the true nature of self being.

World of Illusions

Many Indian religious and spiritual books include the core belief that this world is an illusion, or Maya. Scholars and spiritual practitioners have debated and offered their interpretations of this idea in a variety of ways over the centuries. Ancient Hindu works including the Vedas, Upanishads, and Bhagavad Gita first introduced the idea of Maya, and Buddhist and Jain writings have also touched on it.

The Sanskrit words 'ma', which indicates not, and 'ya', which signifies that, are combined to form the word Maya. The phrase 'Maya' can be interpreted as 'that which is not' as a result. Maya is frequently referred to as an illusion or a curtain that hides our true nature and keeps us mired in a cycle of misery and ignorance. Indian spiritual traditions hold that Maya is the root of all human misery and the origin of all forms of servitude.

Maya is frequently referred to as the Goddess Maya or the divine power of illusion in Hinduism. It is believed that the Goddess Maya is the world's creator and the mother of all creatures. In addition, she is seen as the embodiment of the material universe and the origin of all sensory experiences. The world, according to Hindu texts, is a reflection of the divine will, and everything tangible is really an illusion produced by Maya.

The ancient Hindu teachings known as the Upanishads define Maya as a veil that hides the actual nature of the self. The self, also known as the Atma, is frequently referred to as the core of who we are. The self, according to the Upanishads, is limitless consciousness that transcends time and space.

We identify with our bodies, minds, and senses, and we develop attachments to the material world as a result of Maya's impact. This attachment causes us to suffer and keeps us from understanding who we really are.

The idea of Maya is also covered in the famous Hindu literature known as the Bhagavad Gita. It claims that Maya is the divine force that generates and maintains the world. However, this power is also to blame for our pain and servitude. The Bhagavad Gita teaches that by being detached from the world of things and realising our actual essence as the self, we can defeat Maya. We can escape Maya's illusions and achieve spiritual freedom through spiritual practices like meditation and self-examination.

The idea of shunyata, or emptiness, is sometimes equated with the Buddhist concept of Maya. Buddhist teachings hold that all phenomena lack inherent existence and only have an existence in relation to other phenomena. As a result, the world is a transitory phenomenon that is continually changing rather than a fixed and permanent thing. According to the Buddha, our attachment to the delusion of permanence and our conviction that we are different from the rest of the world are the causes of our suffering.

The ancient Indian religion of Jainism, which places a strong emphasis on non-violence and self-control, also discusses the idea of Maya. The world is a complex system of interdependent and interrelated phenomena, and our activities have an immediate effect on the world around us, in accordance with Jain beliefs.

Karma, which denotes the law of cause and consequence, and the Jain notion of Maya are closely related. By overcoming Maya's illusions and leading a life of non-violence and self-control, Jainism claims that humans can escape the cycle of birth and death.

Many Indian religious and spiritual books include the idea of Maya as a fundamental idea. It alludes to the material world's illusion and the veil that conceals our actual selves. The root of all human suffering is Maya.

This is the reality of our existence that we are still not in that kind of a world or we have failed to create that kind of world where the world will embrace each other, everyone will embrace each other and live in love and joy. The failure is mine, yours and everyone living in this world. When it comes to an army force, a soldier needs to kill the enemy to protect his country. He is not harming anyone for personal pleasure but he is doing his 'karma', his duty to fulfil a larger interest. Today, power and diplomacy have become a necessity.

Hormones play an important role in the regulation of thoughts and emotions in our day-to-day life. There are many experiments done by various scientists in the present era of science and technology, which proves that during the first 25 years of life, one becomes happy as a kid, does sports, and builds bodies in the gym. That's due to the release of hormones called endorphins.

At the age of 25, our body becomes tolerant to endorphins, so to get the same quality of happiness, we need a new high dose, which is fulfilled by the hormone dopamine. It is released when one earns money, earns respect by getting fame. By 50, our body becomes resistant to dopamine. So, one needs high dosage to get happiness, which is fulfilled by serotonin that is released at a high rate when giving money.

Effect of Universe and Cosmos on Individuality

The ocean gives violent waves with high tides during full moon day 'Purnima' due to some symmetrical movements of the moon with respect to earth. The moon is far away from us, still it has an effect on water bodies on earth. If the movement of the moon affects the water bodies on earth, then it also affects the human body because our body consists of 80% water.

Purnima is considered the most important day in various religions. It is believed three important events of Gautama Buddha took place on Purnima—his birth, his attaining enlightenment and his death. Buddhists consider it as BUDDHA PURNIMA. In Hindu and Buddhist culture, the whole fundamental principle of astrology theorems are based on the movement of planets, stars and asteroids.

3.2 Life After Death Cycle

Science and Belief

There is no such reality called death. Life and life alone is the only absolute reality of this universe. This is just the movement and transfer of energy from one dimension to another that we call death. When we say death, the one definition we can consider is to lose this physical body.

There is a meditation in yoga shastra called 'shoonya sadhna', shoonya means nothingness. If someone settles down doing this sadhna, what yogis experience is not near death, it's actually death but conscious death.

When a subject starts its journey, there will come a point it needs to be stopped but this is not the end. For example, if a car starts from a point, then it will stop at a certain destination. Only acceleration is not important, the break is also equally important in reaching the right destination because without breaks, the car will collapse; there will be no destination.

Same with the life system. After the death of an individual, the energy from the body releases into the environment and gets converted and absorbed by other means of nature. Either a tree absorbs the energy of the dead body if buried or it will be converted into some other form if burnt. But the energy remains constant.

Energy can't be created nor destroyed, only can be converted into different forms.

There is nothing to gain and nothing to lose in this life. We came with nothing in hand, whatever the hell is happening, we are on the profit side. We are not allowed to take even a handful of rice with us after death. So, at the end, all that matters is how profound and beautiful the experiences we have in our lifetime.

Everyone became a machine by limiting themselves in every step of their life. We all forget to explore life, thinking to become engineer, doctor, this keeps us busy for 5-7 years. Then comes the struggle for job, which keeps us busy for 3-4 years. Then comes marriage to this girl, that boy who keeps us busy for more than 3-5 years.

Then comes effort to accumulate wealth, which keeps us busy for more 20-25 years. Then children come, expecting them to become this or that. Then with unfulfilled expectations, death knocks at the door. Is this what we call life? Life is a certain combination of space, time and energy.

Life is the limited short period between birth and death. It is a clear reminder that we have limited time and energy. That means we need to organise our time and energy to do 'karma', what is most valuable to us and not to do a single thing more that is not necessary for ourselves and anybody around us.

Desires

In ancient days, somewhere in a village, there was a businessman 'Vaishya', who was running here and there like his tail was on fire. When a monk asked him, he said he needed 1 bag full of gold to start his business. The monk said in a compassionate tone, not to worry, he would provide him the required amount.

The monk instructed the man to meet in his ashram the next day. It was not possible for the business man alone to lift a heavy bag full of gold, so he came with his 5 friends. The monk said very softly, to give 3 bags of gold to each of the five men who had come with him and only 1 bag to the businessman.

He became disappointed and asked, they will get 3 bags of gold. I will get only 1 bag, why? The monk softly enquired, his ambition was to get only 1 bag full of gold, so suddenly what happened?

The whole thing was about having something more than somebody else. That is competition. The dumbest thing in life is the desire to have something more than somebody else and start running hard in the wrong direction to achieve all these fantasies. As a kid competing with others for marks in exams, as a teen competing for a job, as an adult competing for wealth.

This unhealthy competitiveness approach to life will leave us always inadequate, always struggling, always unsatisfied, always panicking, missing out on all the experience of life itself because the only valuable thing we have is our life. Life is to explore with love and joy. Life is not a subject to compete with.

Thus, we need collaboration not competition. In the present world, the problem is everyone is just pushing themselves and even their children into unhealthy competitions with high desires without focusing on competence. We must focus on each individual to enhance their competence, not their ambition.

Everyone has a different skill set and talent. If one enhances their level of competence in their field of interest, at the end, they will do better than what people expect them to do. So, competition will die naturally and organically.

"There's a theory that says that life is based on a competition and the struggle and the fight for survival, and it's interesting because when you look at the fractal character of evolution, it's totally different. It's based on cooperation among the elements in the geometry and not competition."

Bruce Lipton

Life is like a question paper, everyone has different question sets. Even if you succeed in copying answers from others, you will end up failing because no questions are related. Don't ape like others. Discover your own potential.

Immortality Is a Curse

For generations, people have been fascinated by the idea of immortality. The idea of perpetual life has been explored in a variety of contexts, from ancient tales to contemporary science fiction. However, immortality is more often viewed as a punishment than a benefit in many spiritual and religious traditions.

The biblical account of Adam and Eve in the Garden of Eden serves as a warning about the perils of immortality. The Bible claims that Adam and Eve were intended to live forever, but as a result of their transgression, they were driven from the Garden of Eden and put to death. According to this tale, humans were not intended to be immortal, and death is an essential component of the natural order.

Similar to this, Hinduism views moksha, or freedom from the cycle of birth and death, as a desirable endpoint. Because eternal physical immobility would prevent one from ascending to a higher spiritual dimension; immortality is not regarded as the ultimate goal.

The notion of immortality can be viewed as a form of connection to the material world from a spiritual standpoint. We may disregard our soul development and spiritual development if we are fixated on living eternally. The body is viewed as transient in many faiths, whereas the soul is considered everlasting. We risk missing the chance to transcend our physical selves and commune with the divine if we grow overly dependent on them.

In addition, immortality may be perceived as a burden rather than a blessing. In numerous tales, immortal beings are portrayed as lonely and alone, unable to relate to or create meaningful connections with mortal people. Having experienced everything there is to experience and lacking the capacity to develop or evolve, they can also get bored with life.

In conclusion, even though it may seem enticing, immortality is frequently viewed in spiritual and religious traditions as a burden. The desire of eternal life can be understood as a type of connection to the physical world because death and the cycle of birth and rebirth are seen as necessary components of the natural order.

Instead, many faiths teach us to place our attention on the development of our soul and spiritual progress, acknowledging that our physical bodies are but transient containers that will eventually perish. We can develop a greater appreciation for the present moment and a closer relationship with God by accepting the transience of existence.

In Mahabharata, after killing nearly 100 thousand people in those Vedic days when the population was not even 10% of what it is today. Ashwathama didn't stop there; out of his anger, he killed the children of

Pandavas who were sleeping. He went and slit all their throats as revenge for whatever had happened in the Kurukshetra war, which he felt was unfair. Maybe it was unfair but due to what he did, Krishna did not curse him with death, Krishna cursed him with immortality to be in grief and guilt for always.

3.3 Law of Karma

Arrogance and Cosmos

दम्भो दर्पोऽभिमानश्च क्रोधः पारुष्यमेव च |
अज्ञानं चाभिजातस्य पार्थ सम्पदमासुरीम् || 4||

Bhagavad Gita 16:4

"The qualities of those who possess a demonic nature are hypocrisy, arrogance, conceit, anger, harshness, and ignorance."

Everything is interconnected and interdependent in this universe. If it would not be, then life would not be possible. Let's understand with an example, world of flora gives oxygen to fauna and consumes carbon dioxide that is released by fauna. All animals consume oxygen and return carbon dioxide to trees. Trees and animals both are interdependent in nature. One cannot survive without another.

Gravitational forces of different planets and stars gives this universe a perfect balance. Light waves and sound waves from various sources too have an effect on each and every star and planet. Solar radiation has a direct effect of earth and sound waves from space disrupts TV, satellite and mobile communication signals, thus in a macro scale, we are connected with each and every star and planet in this universe.

Nature is a fine example; in response to the greed of human beings, Mother Nature gives natural disasters. Everything you do in macro or micro level, it comes to you directly or indirectly in any form.

That's why Krishna in Bhagavad Gita states to suppress arrogance and encourage complete surrender with love and devotion because nature of arrogance is to give importance only to oneself and not to others. In this system of interconnected universe, arrogance within human disrupts the whole system. That's why Krishna states in Bhagavad Gita to do good karma.

High and Low Level Consciousness

क्लैब्यं मा स्म गमः पार्थ नैतत्त्वय्युपपद्यते |
क्षुद्रं हृदयदौर्बल्यं त्यक्त्वोत्तिष्ठ परन्तप || 3||

Bhagavad Gita 2:3

"O Parth, it is not appropriate for you to yield to this cowardness. Stand and give up this weakness of heart, O vanquisher of enemies."

Analysing Bhagavad Gita, the low level and high level consciousness of human thoughts can be clearly distinguished. Arjuna's consciousness was limited to material benefit, money, kingdom, palace, property and on the other hand, Krishna tries to make Arjuna understand not to run behind material benefit as these are a mere illusion of this universe.

Krishna talks about higher consciousness i.e. name, fame, and respect. This is the difference between different perspectives on life. Krishna has elevated the stage of consciousness to a higher level through his speech in Bhagavad Gita.

सुखदुक्खे समान कृतवा लभलाभौ जयाजयौ
ततो युधाय युज्यस्व निवम पापमवाप्स्यसि

Bhagavad Gita 2:38

"Fight for the sake of duty, treating alike happiness and distress, loss and gain, victory and defeat. Fulfilling your responsibility in this way, you will never incur sin."

There is a limit to achieve lower consciousness material elements but there is no limit to achieve higher consciousness non-material or spiritual elements. All material benefits existing in this universe has a limit but spiritual non-material success doesn't have any limit. For example, employees are afraid of losing jobs but up to a certain time period; after retirement, it doesn't matter.

Unmarried are afraid if at all to get incompatible partner but after marriage, it doesn't matter, he or she just has to move on. But on the other hand, higher consciousness doesn't end. When one gets retired with many properties, then also one is afraid to lose his respect. After marriage, one is afraid if his partner really loves him or not. Respect, love, self-realisation, self-esteem and other elements of spirituality is the component of higher consciousness, it doesn't have any age and limitation.

Your life depends on which level of consciousness regulates your thought. For example, famous scientist APJ Kalam, the missile man of India, someone asked why he had not married till date; he replied that he had never thought of it. Work timely, wisely and rightly to get success in life.

Newton's Third Law states, "every action has an opposite and equal reaction." The same principles governs in real life too. The consequences of every event depends upon the action provided.

Good deeds may be fruitless in short term but always fruitful in the long run and bad deeds may be fruitful in short run but always fruitless in a long-term journey.

Righteousness is Divine Act

यदा यदा हि धर्मस्य ग्लानिर्भवति भारत।
अभ्युत्थानमधर्मस्य तदात्मानं सृजाम्यहम् ॥४-७॥

Bhagavad Gita 4:7

परित्राणाय साधूनां विनाशाय च दुष्कृताम् ।
धर्मसंस्थापनार्थाय सम्भवामि युगे युगे ॥४-८॥

Bhagavad Gita 4:8

"Whenever there is a decline in righteousness and an increase in sinfulness, O Arjun, at that time, I manifest myself on Earth. To protect the righteous, to annihilate the wicked, and to re-establish the principles of dharma, I appear on this Earth, age after age."

कर्मण्येवाधिकारस्ते मा फलेषु कदाचन।
मा कर्मफलहेतुर्भूर्मा ते सङ्गोऽस्त्वकर्मणि॥

Bhagavad Gita 2:47

"Always think about work (karma) because it's in your hand. Don't waste your time in thinking about consequences while doing righteous karma because result is not in your hand."

Good deeds seem to be very easy in theory. There is always a clash between compliance and compassion or favouritism vs meritocracy. It's okay to have emotions but it is wrong to be emotional, it is ok to have sentiments but wrong to become sentimental.

For example, there is a fire fighter whose wife is ill and without treatment may die; he receives a call to rescue 10 people caught in a fire, he will serve his ill wife or go to rescue 10 people? An insurance agent whose house is on mortgage, mother is ill and sisters are to marry, there is urgent need of money, there is only one way he can save his house, with the high commission selling wrong policy to his clients.

If he sells a wrong policy, it's unethical and if he doesn't, his house, mother and sisters are at stake. It's not easy to become ethical. It's always the rarest of the rare in which a teacher with his own hands, will fail his own child in the exam if he is not eligible to pass.

Rarest of rare in which a vice-chancellor or founder rejects his own child admission in college due to low merit marks; rarest of rare in which a judge with his own hands gives a death sentence to his own son and breaks nib of the pen; rarest of rare in which a police officer files a FIR against his own son; rarest of rare in which a heart surgeon will conduct surgery of another urgent case, ignoring his own son's heart operation.

It's natural to choose emotions above ethics but karma stands concrete to all. 'Law of karma' or 'karma yoga' is a very difficult way to achieve salvation.

Forgiveness Is Divine Quality

तेज: क्षमा धृति: शौचमद्रोहोनातिमानिता |
भवन्ति सम्पदं दैवीमभिजातस्य भारत ||

Bhagavad Gita 16:3

"Vigour, an attitude of forgiveness towards others, courage, purity, goodwill, towards others, and freedom from pride. All of these, dear Arjuna, are considered by Me to be the greatest characteristics of a man who possesses a divine nature and has come into this world from heaven."

Why to forgive the enemy and abuser? It's actually hard to forgive.

Understanding Garud Puran, do the easiest thing, don't forgive. Don't struggle hard to forgive somebody. Do what is comfortable for your own. If it is comfortable to not forgive, then its ok. Every day think about them, be furious about them and every morning-night, think about them taking revenge, before going to bed, as soon as you sleep, as soon as you wake up, just struggle with your revengeful thoughts. And just realise how you feel! You are nurturing an abuser and demon inside your brain. Forgiving is not for that person who abuses but it is for our own sake.

Love and Generosity

Love is not just a relationship, it's the sweetness of our emotions. Whether we look at a plant, an animal, a child, hills, ocean or the vast sky, why can't we see everything always lovingly? Because it's not about loving the subject but it's about the sweetness of our emotion at that particular time.

If our emotions are sweet, whatever we look at, we will look in a certain way of love and if our emotions are nasty at that particular instance of time, we look at everything in a different way. Therefore, love is not something that we do, it's something that we can become.

Einstein once said, "Sit with a pretty girl for an hour and it feels like a minute; sit on a hot stove for a minute and it feels like many hours. That's relativity."

Similarly, at a time if we are filled with love, then poison too will seem like nectar but if we are filled with hatred, then nectar will also feel like poison.

इतीरितोऽयं प्रियया क्षुधार्तया जुगुप्समानोऽपि धने मदावहे ।
तदा त्वदालोकनकौतुकाद्ययौ वहन् पटान्ते पृथुकानुपायनम् ॥३॥

Narayaneeyam-Dashaka 87—Sudama (Kuchela)

Shloka 3

त्रपाजुषोऽस्मात् पृथुकं बलादथ प्रगृह्य मुष्टौ सकृदाशिते त्वया।
कृतं कृतं नन्वियतेति संभ्रमाद्रमा किलोपेत्य करं रुरोध ते ॥६

Narayaneeyam-Dashaka 87—Sudama (Kuchela)
Shloka 6

यदि ह्ययाचिष्यमदास्यदच्युतो वदामि भार्यां किमिति व्रजन्नसौ।
त्वदुक्तिलीलास्मितमग्नधी: पुन: क्रमादपश्यन्मणिदीप्रमालयम् ॥८

Narayaneeyam-Dashaka 87—Sudama (Kuchela)
Shloka 8

किं मार्गविभ्रंश इति भ्रमन् क्षणं गृहं प्रविष्ट: स ददर्श वल्लभाम्।
सखीपरीतां मणिहेमभूषितां बुबोध च त्वत्करुणां महाद्भुताम् ॥९॥

Narayaneeyam-Dashaka 87—Sudama (Kuchela)
Shloka 9

Sudama was a poor Brahmin who had a repulsive nature towards wealth, as according to him, it was the root cause of all pride and arrogance. Therefore, when Sudama went to visit Krishna's golden palace, due to poverty, he could not afford anything to gift. So, he brought a pouch of raw grains to offer to Krishna.

When Krishna received the pouch of grains, he ate it with immense joy and pleasure despite Rukmini's objection. Lord Krishna gave away heaven 'swarga lok' to poor Sudama on eating the first handful of rice from the pouch and gave earth 'bhu lok' to Sudama while eating the second handful of rice.

That means now Sudama was the lord of the whole world. But when Krishna was about to take a third handful of rice, he was going to give away heaven 'Vaikunta' where Lakshmi lives. So immediately, Lakshmi stopped Lord Krishna from eating and snatched the whole pouch of raw rice and with her friends, they ate the whole.

Moreover, Krishna made Sudama sit on his golden throne with cushions and washed his feet, as a mark of respect. The whole cosmos witnessed the best example of social-economic-political equality, 'Vasudhaiva

Kutumbakam'. This is the culture of 'DEV BHUMI', 'BHARAT' that preaches generosity.

Also, on the other hand, we get the best life example to distinguish between investment and dana (alms) by analysing Mahabharata. No doubt that Karna was a great warrior, but when Karna was banned to fight with Prince Arjuna by the council (sabha) in rangbhoomi by stating, a 'sutaputra' sudra caste cannot battle with a prince of royal blood, at that moment Duryodhana declared helpless Karna the king of Anga Pradesh, which Karna had never visited in his lifetime.

It was a good investment on the side of Duryodhana as Karna was exploited like a slave in the whole Mahabharata. Literally, Karna was abided and bondaged with the moral obligation of friendship. This is not dana (alms). Dana is done lovingly and affectionately without intention to get anything in return. So, realise the true sense, not every give-away becomes dana (alms).

Philosophy of Candle

In the present world, some good people too help others and render service to others but only up to a limitation. If you have two seats reserved while travelling, one for you and another for your friend who couldn't come due to some reason, and when any other person asks to sit, naturally most of you can give without any objection, even if you have no refund.

But just think, if you have only one seat, how many of us gives away our own seat in the bus or train to old senior citizens while travelling? Often, people quarrel with others for seat preference even in the passenger non-reserved seat category.

Our life has become like cream; that means to enjoy before it melts, enjoy up to the fullest before death but on the other hand, just think how opposite the philosophy of the candle is. The philosophy of candle is to give light to others, burning self before it melts. Both ice-cream melts and candle also melts but the difference is ice-cream is enjoyed before it melts and candle serves others by emitting light before it melts. This is a fine example of selfishness and selflessness.

Thus, most human selfless acts are always in limited course, if at all not affecting one's own selfish interest. Those who sacrifice personal interest for the service of others are the 'karma yogis'. They forget themselves in the service of others. According to yoga, this is karma yoga and it is the most difficult path to achieve 'moksha' or salvation.

Chapter 4

MAGIC AND OCCULT SCIENCE

For millennia, people have been enthralled by magic and occult science. These phrases can be used interchangeably, despite the fact that they typically refer to different practices. Magic is the practice of harnessing mystical or supernatural powers to influence the natural world, whereas occult science is the study of secret or esoteric knowledge.

Philosophy, spirituality, and religion have all in the past been intertwined with occultism and magic. Among the several ancient civilisations that believed in magic and used it in a variety of ways are the Egyptians, Greeks, and Romans. Some civilisations used magic for healing, while others used it for defence or to establish domination over others.

Alchemy and astrology were closely related to the study of esoteric knowledge during the Middle Ages. These techniques were used to understand the natural world and its relationship to the cosmos. Transmutation, or the transformation of one substance into another, was prioritised, particularly in alchemy, sometimes with the goal of creating a substance that would grant immortality.

There was a resurgence of interest in magic and occult study throughout the Renaissance due to the emergence of new religious systems like Hermeticism and Kabbalah. The acquisition of esoteric knowledge and the attainment of spiritual enlightenment are strongly stressed in these practices. Leonardo da Vinci and Isaac Newton were two well-known Renaissance figures who were known to practise these arts.

In the modern era, magic and occult science have undergone substantial transformation. They are employed by persons seeking enlightenment and personal growth and are typically associated with New Age mysticism. Energy work, crystal therapy, and tarot reading are a few instances of contemporary fads that have gained popularity.

Despite their continued allure, magic and occult science have long been viewed with suspicion and contempt. Many cultures regarded the use of magic as evil or demonic, and those who did so, faced persecution. Others saw it as a swindler's trick to take advantage of the gullible.

4.1 Yantra

Hinduism and other Eastern religions use yantras, mystical geometric patterns, for meditation and other spiritual exercises. The Sanskrit words 'yam', which means 'to control' or 'to regulate', and 'tra', which means 'instrument', combine to form the word 'yantra'. Yantras are tools that assist us in maintaining mental and energetic focus on achieving our spiritual objectives.

Spirituality and Yantra

Yantras are said to be effective aids for meditation and spiritual development in Indian mysticism. Yantras are thought to represent cosmic energy and can facilitate spiritual connection for practitioners. According to legend, the geometric shapes found in yantras have a resonant frequency with the energies of the cosmos and can assist practitioners in synchronising their energies with these energies.

In India, yantras are employed in a number of spiritual disciplines including astrology, meditation, and puja (worship). Tantra, a type of spiritual practice that aims to unite the individual consciousness with the global awareness, also employs yantras. The fundamental force known as Kundalini, which is asleep at the base of the spine, is awakened using yantras in tantric practices.

Ayurveda, the conventional Indian medical system, also employs yantras. Yantras are utilised to treat a variety of physical and mental conditions and are thought to have therapeutic abilities.

Yantra and the Occult

The term 'occult' describes knowledge that is obscured or secret and out of reach of the five senses. The occult is frequently linked to mysticism, magic, and the paranormal. Because of their esoteric nature and employment in spiritual practices that are difficult for the average person to understand, yantras are frequently linked to the occult.

The term 'occult' is frequently linked to sorcery and black magic in the

West. The occult is not always connected to evil practices in India, though. In India, the occult is frequently connected to tantra and other esoteric practices and is viewed as a route to enlightenment on a spiritual level.

In occult practices like tantra, yantras are frequently employed to activate the Kundalini energy and establish a connection with the divine. Yantras are also employed in astrology, where they serve to symbolise the energies of the planets. Yantras are thought to be able to channel the energy of the planets, enhancing their beneficial effects while balancing their unfavourable effects.

Mantras, which are sacred sounds or sentences repeated during meditation or worship, are frequently used with yantras in the occult. Mantras are said to have a strong mental influence and can facilitate communication with the divine.

Yantra's Relationship to the Occult

The esoteric nature of both practices is the basis for the relationship between yantra and the occult. The occult is involved with secret information and spiritual practices that are not easily comprehended by the general public, whereas yantras are esoteric symbols that reflect cosmic energy.

Yantras are frequently employed in occult disciplines like tantra and astrology, where they are employed to invoke the divine and channel the power of the planets. The occult is frequently connected to mysticism and magic, and yantras are occasionally used in magical rituals to increase their potency.

It's important to remember, though, that not all yantra practices involve magic or the occult. Yantras can be utilised for spiritual growth and healing, and their application is not confined to the esoteric activities of the occult.

Science Behind Yantra

Resonance is a fundamental idea in both quantum physics and the science of yantra. A phenomenon known as resonance occurs when one thing vibrates in reaction to another object that also vibrates at the same frequency. This is referred to as 'quantum entanglement' in quantum physics, where particles become interconnected to the point where their states are dependent on one another regardless of how far apart they are.

Yantras are composed of various shapes and symbols that are intended to produce a particular resonance with the universe's energy. It is thought that each shape and symbol has a different vibration and frequency that interacts with and shapes the energy of the universe.

One intricate geometric design is the Sri Yantra, which consists of nine interconnecting triangles. It is thought to possess the ability to bring riches, prosperity, and spiritual enlightenment. It is meant to symbolise the cosmic creation of the universe. The Sri Yantra is also supposed to have a particular resonance with the energy of the universe that can assist in bringing a person's ideas and desires into harmony with that energy.

The Mandala Yantra, a circular geometric pattern utilised for meditation and spiritual purposes, is another illustration. The Mandala Yantra is thought to resonate with the person's own energy field and aid in balancing and harmonising it.

The idea of the observer effect is also related to the science underpinning yantra and quantum physics. The act of monitoring a system can alter its behaviour, a phenomenon known as the observer effect. The Heisenberg Uncertainty Principle in quantum physics states that a particle's momentum can change when its position is measured and vice versa.

In yantra, it is said that concentrating on a particular shape or symbol has a similar impact on one's consciousness and energy field. The person can view and control their own energy by concentrating on the yantra, which then allows them to control the energy of the universe.

The theory of non-locality is also related to the science of yantra and quantum physics. No matter how far two particles are from one another, they can be connected through a phenomena known as non-locality in which their states are interdependent. In numerous quantum physics experiments, the concept of 'quantum entanglement' has been proven.

The resonance that the yantra produces is thought to include the idea of non-locality in yantra. It is thought that the energy of the universe is non-local, existing simultaneously everywhere. The yantra is thought to link the individual with the energy of the universe, regardless of where they are in space and time, by generating a resonance with this non-local energy.

The idea of energy fields is also related to the science underpinning yantra and quantum physics. Particles are not only physical things in quantum physics; they are also energy fields. These energy fields have the ability to interact with one another and alter an object's overall energy level.

4.2 Mantra

Mantras are revered sounds, words, or phrases used in a variety of Indian religious and spiritual rituals. Indian culture has a long history of using mantras, and many people think they have a significant impact on the mind, body, and soul. One of the most potent and well-known mantras in Hinduism is the Gayatri mantra in particular.

The Mantra Science

The principles of sound and vibration are the foundation of mantra science. Waves of energy in the form of sound flow through the atmosphere. The frequency and amplitude of these waves, which affects the sound's quality, are particular. Sound waves are produced when particles travel quickly back and forth, or vibrate. A unique pattern of sound waves with a particular frequency and amplitude is produced when we sing a mantra.

Ancient Indian traditions claim that 'Nada Brahma', or sound waves, make up the universe. Accordingly, the human body and the entirety of the cosmos are composed of sound vibrations. By harmonising our frequencies with those of the universe when we say a mantra, we produce a peaceful resonance inside ourselves. Our mind, body, and soul are all profoundly affected by this resonance.

The Gayatri Mantra

One of Hinduism's most potent and well-known mantras is the Gayatri. It is a hymn from the Rigveda, one of Hinduism's earliest sacred books. The sun god Savitr is honoured by the mantra, which is frequently chanted at dawn and dusk. The Gayatri mantra is thought to have the ability to reach enlightenment and awaken the spiritual consciousness.

The Gayatri mantra has a particular rhythm and melody and has 24 syllables. A potent vibration is produced by placing the words in a particular order that resonates with the universe. The mantra is frequently sung in a certain style, with equal emphasis placed on each syllable and a particular tone.

The Gayatri Mantra: The Science

The principles of sound and vibration are the foundation of the science behind the Gayatri mantra. The mantra's precise syllable placement produces a distinctive pattern of sound waves with a certain frequency and amplitude. By repeating the Gayatri mantra, we synchronise our internal resonance with the vibrations of the cosmos.

It is also thought that the Gayatri mantra opens the chakras in the body. The body's energy centres known as chakras are linked to several facets of our physical, emotional, and spiritual health. The Gayatri mantra opens the crown chakra, which is connected to enlightenment and spiritual awakening. A profound sensation of calm, clarity, and connection with the divine can result from this activation.

The Advantages of Gayatri Mantra Chanting

- The mind, body, and spirit can all benefit greatly from reciting the Gayatri mantra. Among the advantages are:
- Increased focus and concentration: The Gayatri mantra might aid with attention and concentration. During meditation, the mantra is frequently used to assist focus the mind and develop awareness.
- Less anxiety and stress: The Gayatri mantra can be used to ease anxiety and stress. Both the mind and the body can be calmed by the mantra's rhythm and melody.
- Increased vitality and energy: Energy and vitality can be increased by reciting the Gayatri mantra. The phrase is thought to open the body's chakras, which can enhance general health and well-being.
- The reawakening and illumination of the spirit: The Gayatri mantra can aid in Kundalini awakening.

4.3 Tantra

Tantra is a term that has been used in a wide variety of contexts throughout history, but in the context of Indian spirituality, it refers to a series of rituals and beliefs that aim to connect the human with the divine by means of a variety of mental and physical practices. Tantra is a vast and varied school of thought that has its origins in India's Vedic era.

Tantra's Origins and History

Tantra's historical roots can be found in India's early Vedic era, which began around 1500 BCE. Vedic religion, which at the time was the country's preeminent spiritual tradition, was distinguished by complex ceremonies and sacrifices that were thought to please the gods and benefit the community.

But as time went on, some people started to doubt the effectiveness of these rites and looked for other ways to commune with the holy. In an effort to reach a higher state of consciousness and a closer relationship with the divine, these seekers opted to ascetic practices including fasting, meditation, and self-mortification.

The tantric tradition, which was characterised by its emphasis on personal experience and utilisation of diverse physical and mental procedures to connect with the divine, was finally born from this novel approach to spirituality.

The sage Yajnavalkya, who is credited with writing the Brihadaranyaka Upanishad, one of the most significant scriptures in the Vedic tradition, was a pivotal player in the creation of tantra. Many of the fundamental ideas and techniques of tantra, such as the use of mantras, visualisations, and various bodily postures and gestures to communicate with the divine, are found in the Brihadaranyaka Upanishad.

Tantra developed into a sophisticated and multifaceted system of thinking over time, giving rise to several sub-traditions and schools of thought. Other religious movements like Buddhism and Jainism, which were thriving in India at the time, had an impact on tantra as well.

Philosophy of Tantra

Tantra is fundamentally a school of thought that employs a variety of mental and physical methods to bring about the union of the person with the divine. Tantra claims that through connecting with this divine essence, people can achieve a higher state of consciousness and a greater relationship with the divine. Tantra asserts that the divine is present in all things.

The idea of the body's many chakras, or energy centres, is one of the foundational ideas of tantra. According to tantra, by activating and balancing these energy centres, people can experience a better feeling of inner harmony and connection to the divine. These energy centres are said to be linked to particular emotions, desires, and parts of the self.

The Kundalini, also known as the snake power, is another key idea in tantra. It is thought to be a dormant force that coils at the base of the spine. People can awaken this energy and raise it through the chakras by various practices including yoga and meditation, which results in a condition of enhanced consciousness and spiritual enlightenment.

In addition to the use of mantras, visualisations, and various physical postures and gestures, tantra practice also incorporates the use of other mental and physical practices. These methods, which frequently include diverse rites and ceremonies, are intended to aid people in focusing their attention and establishing a connection with the divine.

Tantra and Kundalini

Two ideas with a long history in the spiritual and yoga practices of ancient India are Tantra and Kundalini. Several ancient works and scriptures, such as Patanjali's Yoga Sutras and the Bigyan Bhairav Tantra, have examined and elaborated on these ideas.

Although the Patanjali Yoga Sutras don't specifically reference Kundalini, they do touch on the idea of energy in the body. The idea of prana, a vital life stream that runs through the body, is discussed by Patanjali. The goal of pranayama, also known as breath control, is to control this vital force in order to improve health and welfare.

The Bigyan Bhairav Tantra contains an explicit discussion of Kundalini. In order to awaken this dormant energy and direct it through the chakras to achieve a state of spiritual enlightenment, the literature describes a number of practices. These routines include physical activity, chanting, visualisation, and meditation.

The two books' approaches to spiritual enlightenment are one of their most significant contrasts. In order to promote spiritual growth, Patanjali's Yoga Sutras emphasise the eight limbs of yoga (yama, niyama, asana, pranayama, pratyahara, dharana, dhyana, and samadhi). Each of these limbs is regarded as an essential step towards enlightenment.

The Bigyan Bhairav Tantra, on the other hand, has a more eclectic stance and draws on a wide range of procedures and strategies from other spiritual traditions. The value of first-hand experience and trial-and-error in spiritual practice is emphasised in this text. Practitioners are encouraged to explore and experiment with many ways rather than adhere to a predetermined path in order to determine what is most effective for them.

Both scriptures stress the significance of self-awareness and introspection in spiritual development despite these variances. The Patanjali Yoga Sutras place a strong emphasis on meditation as a way to cultivate self-awareness and get a profound insight of the nature of the self. Similar emphasis on meditation, introspection, and the development of mindfulness and awareness in daily life may be found in the Bigyan Bhairav Tantra.

The notion of polarity or duality is another essential tantric principle. Tantra views the world as a dance between opposites, including male and female, positive and negative, and light and dark. Spiritual practice seeks to embrace these dualities and strike a balance between them rather than to transcend them.

The practise of Kundalini yoga, which emphasises the balancing of male and female energies within the body, also reflects this idea. The movements and postures used in Kundalini yoga are frequently directed at energising and balancing these energies.

Ancient Indian literature like Patanjali's Yoga Sutras and the Bigyan Bhairav Tantra have investigated and elaborated on the connections between tantra and Kundalini. Although the two scriptures approach spiritual development in different ways, they both stress the value of self-awareness, introspection, and first-hand experience in gaining spiritual awakening.

In these scriptures, the idea of Kundalini, which denotes a potent force that, when awakened and guided, can result in profound spiritual transformation, is particularly important.

Chapter 5

SUPERNATURAL ABILITIES AND SIDDHIS

In Indian mysticism, supernatural aptitudes, also known as siddhis, are regarded as spiritual attainments. Intense spiritual practice, such as meditation, yoga, and other types of spiritual discipline, is said to be the source of these skills.

In Indian spirituality, siddhis are seen as remarkable abilities that people who have reached a high level of spiritual growth can gain. Clairvoyance, levitation, telekinesis, astral projection, and the capacity to manipulate the elements are reportedly among these skills.

The Hindu and Buddhist traditions of India have a strong hold on the idea of siddhis. The Yoga Sutras of Patanjali, a historic book that covers the eight limbs of yoga, are an ancient scripture that describes siddhis in Hinduism. These siddhis are seen as stepping stones on the road to spiritual liberation and are said to be by-products of doing yoga.

Similar to this, siddhis are seen as accomplishments in Buddhism that emerge from fervent spiritual practice. The Buddhist tradition recognises six supernatural abilities, including the capacity for flight, invisibility, and mind reading.

Siddhis are frequently regarded as desirable in Indian spirituality, but they are not regarded as the ultimate objective. Instead, spiritual freedom, or moksha, is viewed as the ultimate objective and is attained via understanding the underlying essence of reality.

It is significant to highlight that there is disagreement among scientists regarding the reality of siddhis. Although some people claim to have had supernatural experiences, there is no scientific proof to back up the existence of these talents.

Siddhis, as a whole, are a fascinating component of Indian spirituality that has captured the attention of people all over the world for a very long time. While the existence of these powers is in question, many people who are on the road of spiritual development still have their sights set on achieving spiritual emancipation.

5.1 Analysis on Siddhi

It is crucial to remember that the idea of siddhi, or supernatural talents, has a long history in Indian spirituality and can be seen from a variety of angles. The supernatural or paranormal talents that are said to be accessible via spiritual practice or yoga are referred to as siddhi, which is a Sanskrit word meaning perfection or accomplishment. These skills include levitation, telepathy, clairvoyance, and even the capacity to create things out of nothing. Yoga, Tantra, and Ayurveda are just a few of the Indian spiritual practices that place a strong emphasis on siddhis.

Since ancient times, siddhi has played a significant role in Indian mysticism. These skills are thought to have been attained by the ancient yogis and sages after years of diligent spiritual study and meditation. In fact, it is said that numerous prehistoric scriptures, such as the Vedas, Upanishads, and Puranas, contain tales of sages who acquired siddhi and employed them for the benefit of humanity.

However, there has always been scepticism and debate around siddhis. While some individuals think these supernatural skills actually exist, others just think they're superstitions. The science underlying siddhi and whether it may be attained through spiritual practice have recently attracted the attention of scientists and researchers.

Why Siddhi Is Scientific

Siddhis are thought to occur from the awakening of the Kundalini energy, which is claimed to reside at the base of the spine, from a spiritual standpoint. Yoga, meditation, and pranayama (breathing techniques) are some spiritual practices that might help you activate this energy.

The seven chakras, or energy centres, in the body are said to exist in accordance with yogic tradition, and each chakra is connected to a particular siddhi. For instance, the third eye chakra is linked to clairvoyance and the capacity to perceive things that exist beyond of the physical world. The ability to transcend bodily boundaries and levitation are both related to the crown chakra.

These chakras are thought to open as a result of the Kundalini energy awakening, which eventually results in the acquisition of siddhis. The process of arousing the Kundalini energy, however, is not a simple one and necessitates years of persistent practise under the direction of an experienced guru.

The idea of Kundalini energy and chakras can be described scientifically using the concepts of neuroscience and quantum physics. In order to process information and transfer signals throughout the body, the human body possesses a sophisticated network of neurons that together create a neural network, as found by neuroscientists.

The chakras can be considered as energy hubs that correspond to various parts of the brain. For instance, the pineal gland, which is positioned in the middle of the brain and in charge of regulating sleep and circadian cycles, is connected to the third eye chakra. The cerebral cortex, which is in charge of conscious thought and perception, is linked to the crown chakra.

The idea of energy centres in the body is also explained by quantum physics. Everything in the universe, including the human body, is composed of energy, according to quantum theory. The subtle body, which consists of the mind, intellect, and ego, as well as the physical body contain this energy.

By self-controlling the flow of energy within the physical body, one can gain ability to bring a change in energy level of any object outside the body by concentration or meditation.

5.2 Types of Siddhi

There are allegedly eight basic siddhis, each with distinct qualities and advantages. Some of these skills have been studied by contemporary science and might have a scientific explanation, even if many of them may seem fantastical or even impossible to the rational mind.

- Anima: The capacity to reduce one's size and merge with the tiniest particle. In order to obtain insight into the body and mind's true essence, the practitioner of this siddhi is claimed to be able to penetrate even the minutest fissures of them.

Even though it may seem impossible to physically shrink oneself, new work in quantum physics has revealed that particles can exist in two places simultaneously and even communicate with one another over very long distances, seemingly breaking the laws of physics.

One of the eight siddhis, or supernatural abilities, mentioned in Indian spiritual traditions, especially in the Yogic and Tantric scriptures, is Anima siddhi. The term 'Anima siddhi' refers to the power to govern the physical body, mind, and senses while shrinking to the size of an atom or even a subatomic particle.

The idea of Anima siddhi might be understood as a type of psychosomatic metamorphosis from a scientific standpoint. There are many trillions of cells in the human body, and each one has a unique structure and function. Depending on the type of cell, these cells can range in size from a few micrometres to several centimetres. It is possible to change the behaviour of individual cells and, in turn, the size of the body by learning to control the functioning of the body and mind via spiritual practice and meditation.

Recent studies in the field of epigenetics have demonstrated that meditation and other spiritual practices can affect how genes are expressed, resulting in modifications to the physiology and behaviour of the body. For instance, research has demonstrated that meditation can boost telomerase activity, an enzyme that fixes the ends of chromosomes, resulting in better cellular health and longevity. According to other research, meditation can help people feel less stressed and anxious, which enhances their general health and well-being.

In a broader sense, Anima siddhi can also be seen as a metaphor for how everything in the universe is interrelated. Indian spiritual traditions assert that everything in the cosmos is interrelated and that realising this connection and uniting with the universe is the ultimate objective of spiritual practice. It is possible to directly experience this connectivity through spiritual practice, leading to a sense of oneness with the universe, by learning to manage the body and mind.

According to Indian spiritual traditions, strong yogic practices, like as meditation, pranayama (breathing exercises), and other physical and mental disciplines, are required to obtain Anima siddhi. These exercises are meant to balance and purify the body, mind, and soul as well as enhance focus and visualisation abilities.

The idea of quantum physics, which describes the behaviour of subatomic particles, provides the scientific justification for Anima siddhi. This hypothesis states that all matter in the cosmos is composed of minute particles with wave-like characteristics that are constantly moving and interacting with one another.

Through concentrated intention and visualisation, the yogi is supposed to be able to regulate the motions and interactions of these subatomic particles in the instance of Anima siddhi. They are able to affect the physical universe at a quantum level by focusing their consciousness at the lowest possible level.

Indian spiritual traditions have characterised the concept of Anima siddhi as a superhuman ability that allows a yogi to shrink to the size of an atom or subatomic particle and to have control over the physical body, intellect, and senses. The principles of quantum mechanics, which govern the behaviour of subatomic particles, are the foundation of the scientific explanation for this phenomenon, even though it is still entirely speculative.

- Mahima: The capacity to enlarge oneself to the size of the largest object. According to legend, this siddhi enables the practitioner to transcend physical constraints and have access to the unlimited potential of the cosmos.

One of the eight yogic powers or siddhis that the Indian spiritual tradition describes is the Mahima siddhi. It alludes to the capacity to enlarge oneself or grow to the appropriate size. According to legend, this power can be acquired through arduous meditation and spiritual practices.

The science underlying Mahima siddhi is founded on an understanding of the subtle energies or forces that operate in the universe in the Indian context. Everything in the universe, according to Indian spiritual texts, is composed of the five elements—earth, water, fire, air, and space. The pranas, also referred to as the life force, are the subtle energies or forces that control these elements.

These subtle energies exist within the human body and are intended to be awakened and utilised via the practise of yoga and meditation. It is thought that the practitioner's capacity to influence and regulate these energies leads to the development of Mahima siddhi. It is claimed that a practitioner can alter their form or enlarge themselves by concentrating their energy and intention.

The concept of Maya, or illusion, is related to the science underpinning Mahima siddhi. The physical world is regarded as an illusion or mental projection in the Indian spiritual tradition. A practitioner can transcend the constraints of the physical world and accomplish seemingly miraculous acts like Mahima siddhi by developing mental control.

Mahima siddhi can be explained scientifically in terms of the mind-body link and the power of visualisation. The human body is capable of amazing feats of strength and endurance, but these prowess are frequently constrained by the individual's ideas and views. Individuals have the ability to access a higher degree of physical capability and pull off seemingly unachievable tasks by altering their thoughts and mental state.

The idea of neuroplasticity, which refers to the brain's capacity to modify and adapt in response to experience, can be used to comprehend this phenomenon. People may be able to stimulate neural pathways and fortify the connections between the brain and body by using visualisation techniques and mentally simulating the act of enlarging their size, which would likely result in improved physical capabilities.

Yoga and meditation, which are frequently linked to the growth of siddhis, have also been proven to offer a wealth of positive psychological and physical effects. These techniques can strengthen the immune system, lessen stress and anxiety, and advance general health and well-being.

People may be able to reach their full potential and accomplish incredible feats like Mahima siddhi by developing a deeper awareness of the mind-body link and using relaxation and mental focus practices.

It is crucial to understand that achieving Mahima siddhi is not the end goal of spiritual practice. Instead, it is regarded as a result of the spiritual path leading to enlightenment or self-realisation. The Indian spiritual tradition places a strong emphasis on employing these siddhis for the good of others rather than one's own ego or personal gain.

Understanding and control of subtle energies in the universe and the human body are the foundation of the science of Mahima siddhi. It is the outcome of arduous spiritual training and meditation intended to activate and tame these forces. Although it is a great skill, it should be used for the good of others since it is not the ultimate purpose of spiritual practice.

Even while it may seem difficult to physically enlarge oneself, current research on the universe's expansion suggests that the universe is expanding and that this growth is accelerating at an increasing rate.

- Garima: The capacity to increase one's weight and immobility indefinitely. The practitioner of this siddhi is claimed to be able to ground themselves in the present and get a greater comprehension of the nature of existence.

Even while it may seem impossible to become indefinitely heavy, current study into the relationship between mass and gravity has led to the possibility that this force is connected to the curvature of space-time.

According to science, Garima siddhi is a more developed type of psychokinesis, the capacity to control physical objects with the force of the mind. All matter, according to quantum theory, is composed of energy and vibrations. Therefore, with focused mental energy, highly skilled individuals can change the vibrational frequency of their own bodies and the objects around them.

The exceptional skills displayed by yogis and sages in numerous recorded examples can be linked to Garima siddhi. Neem Karoli Baba, a well-known Indian saint, was reputed to be able to levitate, make himself enormously heavy or light, and execute other amazing deeds.

Scientific research has also been done on people who claim to have psychokinetic talents, such as the capacity to change the weight of things. Although these trials' findings were ambiguous, there is evidence that some people might indeed have psychokinetic powers.

- Laghima: The capacity to levitate and float through the air. According to legend, this siddhi enables the practitioner to reach spiritual enlightenment and access higher levels of awareness.

In Indian spiritual and yogic traditions, the capacity to become light in weight or weightless is referred to as Laghima siddhi. These traditions claim that it is one of the eight siddhis, or supernatural abilities, attained via rigorous spiritual exercises including meditation, pranayama, and yoga.

Laghima siddhi can be described in terms of the connection between consciousness and gravity from a scientific standpoint. All objects with mass are affected by gravity, a fundamental force of nature, which causes them to gravitate towards one another. Consciousness, on the other hand, is a non-material part of human experience that defies the laws of science.

According to some current physics theories, including string theory and quantum mechanics, consciousness can affect the behaviour of matter and energy at the subatomic level. This raises the possibility that awareness is capable of influencing gravitational forces and changing the body's weight.

According to Indian spirituality, achieving Laghima siddhi entails having a thorough grasp of the mind-body link and the ability to transcend the constraints of the physical body via spiritual practice. It is believed to be an uncommon and sophisticated level of spiritual development that needs years of dedicated practise.

In conclusion, the idea of Laghima siddhi highlights the possible connection between awareness and the fundamental forces of nature and serves as a link between science and spirituality. The spiritual traditions of India provide a rich and exciting framework for studying the mysteries of the human mind and its potential for good, even when the scientific reason for this phenomenon may not yet be fully understood.

Even though it may appear impossible to be weightless, current studies on the nature of gravity and the behaviour of subatomic particles have led to the hypothesis that particles can exist in a state of superposition, seemingly defying the laws of physics.

- Prapti: The capacity to teleport to any place in the cosmos is known as Prapti. The practitioner of this siddhi is supposed to be able to access higher planes of reality and transcend the confines of time and space.

While it may seem implausible to be able to teleport oneself, current research on quantum entanglement suggests that particles can be connected in ways that cause their properties to instantly coincide, seemingly violating the laws of physics.

Prapti siddhi is one of the eight main abilities or 'siddhis' gained by spiritual practices in Indian mysticism. It alludes to the power to quickly manifest any desired object or thing without the use of physical methods or effort. Prapti denotes achievement, while siddhi denotes perfection.

The concept of manifestation or the law of attraction can be used to scientifically explain the Prapti siddhi occurrence. This idea holds that energy and vibrations make up everything in the universe. Additionally, the vibrations and frequencies that our thoughts, feelings, and beliefs produce draw in other vibrations and frequencies from the universe.

By harmonising our frequencies with the vibrations of what we want, we can manifest anything since our ideas and emotions shape the reality we experience. The 'like attracts like' principle is what is used to describe this.

Training the mind to focus and align with the desired target or result is a component of Prapti siddhi practice. This is possible through spiritual practices like meditation, visualisation, affirmations, and others that help elevate our vibrations and produce a positive energy environment.

The cosmos responds by making the desired object or consequence a reality once the mind is focused on it. Depending on the object's complexity or the degree of alignment, this can happen right away or take some time.

The manifestation of a desired object or result through the alignment of our thoughts, emotions, and vibrations with what we want is, in essence, the scientific explanation of Prapti siddhi. Spiritual practices that help us raise our vibrations and produce a positive energy field, which results in the manifestation of our desires, can help us attain this phenomenon.

- Prakamya: The capacity to grant any wish. According to legend, this siddhi enables its user to realise both their material and spiritual goals as well as their deepest aspirations.

Even if it may seem hard to achieve one's goals, current studies on the placebo effect and the power of purpose have shown that the mind has a significant impact on both our physical well-being and the environment in which we live.

In Indian spiritual and occult practices, the term Prakamya siddhi refers to the capacity to bring about one's wants via the force of purpose and focus. One of the eight basic siddhis—supernatural abilities—that can be achieved via spiritual exercises like meditation, yoga, and tantra is this siddhi.

The ability of the mind to affect physical reality can be used to define the Prakamya siddhi idea from a scientific standpoint. The intricate structure of the human mind produces thoughts, feelings, and goals that can have a significant influence on the physical body and the environment.

Recent research in the disciplines of neuroscience and quantum physics has demonstrated that the mind has the capacity to influence reality through the use of observation and purpose. The observer effect is a phenomena where an object or phenomenon's behaviour can change just by being seen. The placebo effect serves as an example of how the power of intention may affect the behaviour of physical systems.

The Indian practice of Prakamya siddhi entails concentrating one's mind on a particular desire or goal and vividly visualising its accomplishment. This focused mental energy can bring about the desired result in the physical world with continued practise. Although this occurrence is sometimes linked to supernatural or heavenly forces, it can alternatively be explained as a manifestation of the mind's fundamental capacity to shape reality.

Overall, the idea of Prakamya siddhi reflects a fusion of spiritual practices with knowledge of the mind-body relationship from a scientific perspective. The potential to bring one's desires into being via focused purpose may appear arcane and mysterious, but it is a trait shared by all people that can be developed with dedication and mental training.

- Isitva: The capacity to master every facet of the physical world. The practitioner of this siddhi is supposed to be able to dominate their physical reality and fully control the material universe.

While it may seem difficult to control everything in the physical world, recent studies on the nature of reality and the power of the mind have shown evidence that our perceptions of reality may be altered by our ideas and beliefs.

'Isitva siddhi' is a term used in Indian philosophy and spirituality to describe achieving a position of ultimate lordship or dominance. One of the eight siddhis (powers) that can be obtained via rigorous spiritual study and meditation is thought to be this one.

Isitva siddhi can be viewed from a scientific standpoint as the outcome of the brain's adaptability. The brain's capacity to adapt and reorganise its neural networks in response to experience and learning is known as neuroplasticity. The brain is rewired to strengthen its capacity for attention, focus, and self-awareness through prolonged meditation and spiritual practice.

Isitva siddhi, as it is known in Indian mysticism, is thought to be attained by a profound comprehension of the interconnectedness of all things and the recognition that one's actual nature is not distinct from the cosmos. One obtains the ability to govern and affect the outside world by achieving this state of consciousness.

This can be explained scientifically as the growth of a strong sense of self-awareness and the capacity to control one's emotions and ideas. Individuals are able to exert more control over their behaviours and reactions thanks to this increased awareness, which results in a feeling of mastery over the outside environment.

Isitva siddhi is often regarded as combining both spiritual and empirical concepts. People can rewire their brains and gain more control over their internal and external experiences through spiritual practices that emphasise self-awareness and concentration, which can result in a feeling of ultimate lordship or ruler ship.

- Vashitva is the power to rule over all living things. The practitioner of this siddhi is supposed to be able to master all living things and fully control the natural universe.

Indian spirituality uses the term 'Vashitva siddhi' to describe the capacity to exert control over one's own and other people's minds. The name is derived from the Sanskrit terms 'vashitva' and 'siddhi', which both imply accomplishment or perfection and control, respectively.

According to science, Vashitva siddhi is the capacity to influence brainwaves and mental states through the power of meditation and concentrated attention. Theta, delta, and other types of brainwaves are produced by the brain, and each is connected to a particular mental state.

One can develop the ability to control these brainwaves by frequent meditation and concentration practise, which results in a state of enhanced awareness and mental control. This enhanced level of awareness is linked to a reduction in stress and anxiety, an improvement in cognitive performance, and an improvement in general well-being.

Additionally, the phenomena of mirror neurons can be used to explain the power of Vashitva siddhi, which is the capacity to affect other people's minds. Our capacity for empathy and understanding other people's actions and feelings is a result of these neurons. One can learn to affect the thoughts and actions of others by acquiring heightened sensitivity to these mirror neurons, which results in a feeling of control and interpersonal interaction mastery.

The ability to exert influence over one's own and other people's minds through the use of meditation, concentration, and knowledge of mirror neurons is known as Vashitva siddhi. This idea has been a cornerstone of Indian mysticism, and contemporary science is now investigating and validating it.

While it may seem impossible to have complete control over all living things, new studies on the interconnectivity of all living things and the power of intention have shown that our thoughts and actions can have a significant impact on other people. Everybody is involved in the thought process.

5.3 How to Attain Siddhis

For thousands of years, people have utilised meditation as a way to unwind, alleviate stress, and improve their general well-being. There are numerous ways to meditate, and various religions and philosophical traditions each have their own special approaches. The Patanjali Yoga Sutra and the Bhairava Tantra are two well-known writings that offer advice on meditation techniques.

A traditional yoga treatise called the Patanjali Yoga Sutra was created by the sage Patanjali over 2,000 years ago. The 196 sutras, or aphorisms, in the text describe the tenets and asanas of yoga. The Yoga Sutra's second chapter, Sadhana Pada, offers instructions on how to practise yoga, including meditation. The Yoga Sutra lists several important meditation techniques, including the following:

In the meditative absorption known as Samadhi, the mind is entirely united and focused. In accordance with Patanjali's Yoga Sutras, Samadhi is reached through eight steps or limbs. Ashtanga Yoga is the name given to these eight steps as a whole.

- Yama: Practising Yama, or moral constraints like non-violence, honesty, non-stealing, celibacy, and non-possessiveness, is the first stage. The mind can focus more easily when these limitations are used to create a calm and pleasant environment.
- Niyama: The next step is to put niyama into practice, which is the Sanskrit term for individual observances including cleanliness, contentment, self-control, self-study, and submission to a higher power. Niyama practice aids in developing a sense of inner discipline and purity.
- Asana: Practise Asana, often known as physical postures, as the third step. Asanas encourage physical health and flexibility while helping to get the body ready for meditation.
- Pranayama: Exercise breath control techniques known as Pranayama in

the fourth level. The mind is calmed and the body's prana (life force) flow is controlled by Pranayama.

- Pratyahara: Often known as the withdrawal of the senses, it is the fifth phase. The mind can concentrate more intently on internal experiences by removing the senses from outward stimuli.
- Dharana: The sixth phase entails engaging in dharana, or concentration. When practising Dharana, the mind is fixed on a single thing or awareness, like a mantra or the breath.
- Dhyana: The seventh phase entails engaging in dhyana, or meditation. In Dhyana, the feeling of self is transcended as the mind is totally engrossed in the subject of concentration.
- Samadhi: Also known as contemplative enlightenment or absorption, is the eighth and final phase. The meditator enters a state of pure consciousness and oneness with God when in Samadhi.

A practitioner can gradually develop the mental and physical prerequisites for Samadhi by adhering to these eight steps.

Another ancient source that offers instructions on meditation methods is the Bhairava Tantra. It is a compilation of the 112 meditation practices that Lord Shiva instructed Devi Parvati in. The methods are intended to assist users in connecting with the divine and drawing upon their own inner wisdom. The Bhairava Tantra mentions several important meditation techniques, including the following:

- Breath awareness entails paying attention to and studying the breath's natural flow in the mind. The goal is to train inner stillness and calm the mind.
- Mantra repetition: This includes mindfully repeating a sacred sound or word, such as 'Om' or 'Aum', with intention. A frequency that encourages inner peace and relaxation is what is intended to be created within the body and mind.
- Visualisation entails forming and holding in the mind's eye an image of a certain object or scenario. The objective is to develop inner creativity

and access the power of the imagination.

In conclusion, there are many ways to meditate, and diverse religions and philosophical traditions all have their own special ways of doing it. The Bhairava Tantra and the Patanjali Yoga Sutra are two well-known writings that offer advice on different meditation techniques. One can learn more about the mind by investigating and putting these techniques to use, which will help them arrive at a condition of inner harmony and calm.

Mystics Yogis

The spiritual practices of mystic yogis are highly regarded in India since they are said to result in oneness with the divine in the end and higher levels of consciousness. These yogis are supposed to have developed supernatural abilities as a result of their strict devotion to their practise.

In India, there are several first-hand accounts of the might of mystic yogis. Sadhguru Jaggi Vasudev, a well-known spiritual figure and the creator of the Isha Foundation, is one such witness. Sadhguru has talked about his encounters with mystic yogis and their amazing skills.

Mystic yogis, according to Sadhguru, have control over their breathing, heart rate, and body temperature. They are also capable of amazing power and endurance feats, such as holding their breath underwater for prolonged periods of time or remaining still for long periods of time.

Dr Dean Radin, a researcher and scientist in the parapsychology field, is another person who has witnessed the power of mystic yogis. Yoga practitioners are able to manage their autonomic nerve system, which controls body processes like heart rate and blood pressure, according to Dr Radin's investigations on the subject.

Indian mythology and tradition are also filled with tales about mystic yogis and their amazing abilities. For instance, the sage Durvasa was reputed to have a fiery temper and the power to curse those who incensed him, while the sage Vishwamitra was claimed to have created the entire cosmos via his skills of meditation.

In general, India's mystic yogis are an amazing and inspiring aspect of the nation's spiritual tradition. People all over the world are captivated and inspired by their extraordinary talents and dedication to their craft. Yoga practitioners are known as yogis, and they use a variety of techniques, such as meditation, breathing exercises, and physical postures, to try to enlighten their spiritual selves. Because of their advanced state of spiritual growth, certain yogis are considered to have attained siddhis, or supernatural abilities.

According to yogic philosophy, siddhis are thought to develop as a result of cultivating particular virtues like devotion, self-control, and mental purity. Though they are seen as a result of spiritual development, the siddhis are not the ultimate aim of yoga. There are numerous accounts of yogis who have displayed exceptional talents or siddhis. The most well-known yogis who possess siddhis are:

Rusi Patanjali

'Patanjali: The Yoga Sutras', a fundamental literature on the practise of yoga, is credited to the ancient Indian sage Patanjali. Legend has it that Patanjali could levitate and could spend long periods of time submerged underwater.

Ancient Indian sage and philosopher Patanjali is renowned for his role in the creation of the yoga philosophy. Although there is some disagreement among academics over his precise birth and death dates, he is thought to have lived in the period between 200 and 300 BCE.

The Yoga Sutras, one of the most significant works on yoga philosophy, was written by Patanjali. A collection of proverbs known as the Yoga Sutras describes the yoga philosophy and practise. There are four chapters in the text, each of which covers a different component of yoga.

One of the main ideas covered in the Yoga Sutras is 'chitta vritti nirodha', which can be loosely translated as 'the cessation of the fluctuations of the mind'. The mind is said to be in a permanent state of flux, shifting from one thought to another, according to Patanjali. In addition to causing discomfort, this continual mental activity makes one feel cut off from reality's fundamental nature.

Patanjali asserts that one must practise yoga, which entails training the mind and body using a number of practices, such as asana (postures), pranayama (breathing exercises), and meditation, in order to transcend this suffering. One can acquire a level of inner peace and freedom from pain by engaging in yoga practise.

Patanjali is renowned for emphasising the value of moral conduct in the practise of yoga. The yamas and niyamas, which he defines, are a set of moral precepts that include things like non-violence, honesty, purity, contentment, and self-discipline.

In addition to his yoga teachings, Patanjali is respected in the Hindu tradition as a mystic and a saint. He is thought to have gained enlightenment and had a personal encounter with God. Yoga practitioners and spiritual searchers all across the world are still studying and putting his teachings and writings into practise.

Swami Rama

The Himalayan Institute was established in Pennsylvania by the well-known yoga master Swami Rama. The capacity to voluntarily control his heartbeat, body temperature, and brainwaves was among the siddhis he was reported to have attained.

In 1925, Swami Rama, a well-known yogi, researcher, and spiritual guide, was born in northern India. He trained and practised under a number of spiritual gurus before opening the Himalayan Institute in Pennsylvania, USA, where he instructed thousands of students from all over the world in yoga, meditation, and philosophy.

One of Swami Rama's most well-known manifestations of his mystical abilities was his capacity to regulate his physiological processes, including heartbeat, respiration, and body temperature. In several scientific studies carried out by academics at universities and healthcare facilities around the world, he exhibited these skills.

Swami Rama was able to elevate the temperature of one hand by a number of degrees while maintaining the temperature of his other hand constant during one such experiment at the Menninger Foundation in

Kansas, USA. He also displayed the capacity to slow down his breathing and heart rate to previously unthinkable levels.

Swami Rama's mystical abilities also included the capacity to perceive others' feelings and thoughts. His disciples and followers said that he had the ability to intuitively perceive their deepest thoughts and emotions and then provide support and guidance in accordance. Additionally, he was reported to possess the capacity to heal others through the power of his mind or touch.

Swami Rama was well-known for his tremendous spiritual accomplishments in addition to these abilities. He reportedly experienced the ultimate reality, or Brahman, first-hand and had acquired several phases of samadhi (meditative absorption), according to his teachers and followers.

Overall, Swami Rama's mystical abilities and spiritual accomplishments have been reported on and documented by a large number of persons and organisations, and they continue to astound and inspire people all over the world.

Paramahansa Yogananda

The Self-Realisation Fellowship was started by the spiritual teacher and novelist Paramahansa Yogananda. He was supposed to have possessed a variety of siddhis, such as the capacity to create things out of nothing, make himself visible or invisible at command, and read the thoughts of others.

Millions of Westerners first learned about yoga and meditation from the highly regarded Indian yogi and spiritual teacher Paramahansa Yogananda. He is renowned for his mystical encounters and amazing abilities, which he employed to inspire and change the lives of his disciples and students.

The tale of Yogananda bringing a dead man back to life is among the most well-known examples of his psychic abilities. During Yogananda's trip to the US in the early 1920s, this incidence occurred. Yogananda was giving a lecture one day in Los Angeles when all of a sudden, he received word that one of his long time students had passed away from a heart attack. Yogananda hurried over to the man's house right away and discovered the lifeless body there.

Yogananda took a seat next to the body and began to meditate. He then started to chant and pray, calling upon the heavenly force to revive the guy. Yogananda remained in deep meditation for some minutes when he abruptly opened his eyes and yelled the man's name. The man slowly opened his eyes and sat up, cognizant and alert to everyone's shock. Through the remarkable abilities of Yogananda's spiritual practice, he had been brought back to life.

Another tale about Yogananda's magical abilities originates from his years spent in India learning under his master, Sri Yukteswar. Yogananda and his teacher happened upon a group of peasants who were lamenting the loss of a little girl who had perished from a snake bite one day as they were strolling in the countryside. Yogananda's guru saw at once that the girl was not actually dead but rather unconscious.

Maharshi Ramana

A well-known Indian sage named Ramana Maharshi lived in the first half of the 20th century. He was respected for both his profound understanding of the essence of reality and his teachings on self-inquiry. He was also renowned for his psychic abilities, which he frequently displayed.

The tale of Ramana Maharshi's meeting with a poisonous cobra is among the most well-known accounts of his mystic abilities. The legend states that one day when he was doing meditation in his cave, a cobra materialised and walked over to him. Ramana Maharshi didn't panic; he kept his head down and his body steady. The sage was still, his eyes closed, in deep meditation as the snake climbed up and wrapped itself around his neck.

The snake untied itself and slithered away after a little while. The cobra was known to be dangerous, and Ramana Maharshi could have easily been bitten, thus the onlookers who saw this were astounded and terrified. The sage was unscathed, though, and it was assumed that his mystical abilities had shielded him from harm.

Ramana Maharshi's prowess as a mystic healer is the subject of another legend. People who sought his assistance for a variety of ailments are said to have done so on numerous occasions, and he was able to cure them by simply putting his hand on their heads or by looking at them. In one case, a patient who had been battling a long-term disease visited him. The moment Ramana Maharshi put his hand on the man's head, he felt better. He lived a long and healthy life once his ailment was entirely cured.

These are just a few instances of the mystical abilities attributed to Ramana Maharshi. He was reputed to be able to read minds, foresee the future, and have profound insights into the essence of existence. His legacy as a mystic and sage remains to this day, and his teachings and life continue to inspire people all over the world.

Sri Yukteshwar

Lahiri Mahasaya, a well-known Indian saint, was a student of Sri Yukteswar, a spiritual guide and novelist. It was claimed that he had siddhis, including the capacity to interact with spiritual creatures and predict the future.

Sri Yukteswar went over to the girl and touched her forehead without hesitation. He then started chanting a mantra, requesting divine intervention to heal the girl and restore her awareness. The girl suddenly opened her eyes and sat up after chanting for a while, completely cognizant and aware. Many of the people started to follow Sri Yukteswar and Yogananda as their spiritual guides after being impressed and thankful to them.

Sri Yukteswar was a revered Indian guru noted for his profound spiritual understanding and magical prowess. His encounters with his student, Paramahansa Yogananda, are the source of one of the most well-known tales concerning his magical abilities.

'Autobiography of a Yogi', Yogananda's autobiography, claims that Sri Yukteswar showed astounding accuracy in his ability to predict the future. Yogananda once questioned Sri Yukteswar about a future occurrence that was scheduled to occur. In response, Sri Yukteswar said that he was unable to give him a specific response right away but that he will be able to in a few days.

Three days later, Yogananda was summoned to Sri Yukteswar's room and informed that the event he had inquired about would really occur as foretold. Yogananda was perplexed and questioned how Sri Yukteswar could be so knowledgeable. In response, Sri Yukteswar said that he could observe how things were developing in the subtle realms of consciousness and that those realms already knew what would happen.

In addition to his propensity for predicting the future, Sri Yukteswar was renowned for his spiritual healing abilities. Yogananda recounts a case in which Sri Yukteswar cured a woman who had tuberculosis. The woman was instantly healed of her condition after Sri Yukteswar touched her forehead.

Sri Yukteswar was renowned for his capacity to speak with entities in higher awareness realms. Sri Yukteswar once spoke with a being from a higher dimension of existence, according to Yogananda. The being informed Sri Yukteswar that a significant spiritual evolution was about to take place for humanity and that he had been sent to aid in this development.

Overall, the spiritual community was aware of and revered Sri Yukteswar's supernatural abilities. He made use of his gifts to uplift people and spread the word about spiritual progress and awakening.

The mystical abilities and spiritual insights that Paramahansa Yogananda possessed are illustrated by a handful of these tales. Yogananda continues to inspire and transform people's lives via his teachings and example, and his legacy shines as a beacon of light in the contemporary world's spiritual landscape.

Baba Hari Das

Baba Hari Das was an Indian yogi who established the Mount Madonna Centre in California while residing in the United States. He was reported to have acquired siddhis, including the capacity to control his body functions, stop his heartbeat, and view faraway objects.

Famous yogi and spiritual teacher Baba Hari Das lived in the 20th century. He was renowned for his extraordinary spiritual gifts and his capacity for doing wonders. He encountered a poisonous snake in one of the most well-known tales of his paranormal abilities.

According to the legend, Baba Hari Das discovered a poisonous cobra while out on a walk in the forest. When the cobra became enraged and was prepared to strike, Baba Hari Das chose to chant a mantra instead of fleeing or attempting to kill the snake. The snake paused in its tracks and started to swing back and forth to the beat of the mantra, appearing to be mesmerised by his chanting.

For several minutes, Baba Hari Das chanted, and at that time, the cobra relaxed more and more. The snake eventually dropped to the ground at his feet, entirely at ease. The cobra was then given a gentle pat on the head by Baba Hari Das, who also spoke to it in a soothing tone, warning it not to hurt anyone and to return to the forest.

The snake slowly stood up and slithered back into the forest, much to the surprise of everyone present. It never once attempted to bite Baba Hari Das. This incident revealed Baba Hari Das's spiritual practice's immense power and his capacity to converse with even the most hazardous of beasts.

Baba Neem Karoli Ji

Baba Neem Karoli Ji, popularly referred to as Neem Karoli Baba, was a revered Indian mystic and spiritual master noted for both his extraordinary abilities and his life-changing teachings. One of the most well-known legends regarding his mystical abilities includes his capacity to create tangible items out of nothing.

One of the most well-known anecdotes of Baba Neem Karoli Ji's power to manifest things includes a devotee who came to see him with a broken watch. There are many accounts of Baba Neem Karoli Ji's power to manifest things. A jeweller had informed the devotee that the watch couldn't be fixed and that he would have to buy a new one.

But when the devotee handed Baba Neem Karoli Ji the broken watch, the Baba snatched it away, shut his eyes, and started to meditate. After sometime, he opened his eyes and gave the devotee his fully repaired and functional watch.

Another well-known tale concerns a follower who brought a damaged camera to see Baba Neem Karoli Ji. Days had passed while the devotee tried in vain to fix the camera. When Baba Neem Karoli Ji took the devotee's camera, he opened it up and took out a small piece of paper. The camera operated well once he shut it and gave it back to the devotee.

These accounts and numerous others show Baba Neem Karoli Ji's capacity for working wonders and connecting with universal energy. Even today, his example and lessons continue to motivate people all around the world. There are numerous more accounts of Baba Hari Das's mystical abilities, such as his skill for prophecy and his gift of healing, as well as his potential to levitate.

However, this encounter with the cobra is still among the most potent and motivational instances of his spiritual prowess. It is crucial to remember that, despite their impressiveness, siddhis are not yoga's ultimate objective. Yoga's main goal is to bring about spiritual emancipation and a condition of oneness with the divine.

Swami Vivekananda

India's most revered mystic and spiritual figure, Swami Vivekananda, lived from 1863 to 1902. One of the most important intellectuals of contemporary India, he played a significant role in bringing the teachings of Vedanta and Yoga to the West.

The Maharaja of Khetri's saga:

Once, Swami Vivekananda went to see the Maharaja of Khetri, who had a terrible headache. The Maharaja had tried a variety of cures, but nothing had been effective. Swami Vivekananda put his palm on the Maharaja's forehead and chanted a mantra when he saw him. The headache quickly subsided, and the Maharaja was fully recovered within a short while.

The mother and kid's tale:

Swami Vivekananda once saw a mother on a train who was very concerned about her ill child. The mother feared the child might not make it through the trip because he had a high temperature. Swami Vivekananda sat next to the youngster and offered to assist. He touched the child's forehead and recited a mantra while doing so. The child's temperature quickly subsided, and he soon drifted off to sleep. The mother was astonished and appreciative.

The cobra's tale:

Swami Vivekananda was once relaxing in the garden when a cobra slithered up to him. Though Swami Vivekananda was requested to leave by the terrified crowd, he refused. The cobra walked up to him and encircled his neck. Swami Vivekananda kept still and carried on with his meditation.

The snake untied itself and slithered away after a little while. Everyone was astounded and enquired as to how he had maintained his composure in the face of peril. In response, Swami Vivekananda said he was fearless because he recognised the divine in all things.

These are just a few instances of Swami Vivekananda's mystic abilities. He had the power to heal and change the lives of those around him and was a great master of yoga and Vedanta. People all across the world are still inspired and guided by his teachings today.

CONCLUSION

We can make certain inferences regarding the creator after studying the subjects of quantum theory, cosmology, metaphysics, and biophysics. It is claimed that the divine being known as God is a manifestation of the energy that permeates our surroundings. The three parts of God—Brahma, Vishnu, and Mahesh—representing creation, preservation, and destruction are said to exist in the old texts.

The yoga shastra gives strategies to encounter God and energy as well as insights into the existence of spirits and the soul. It emphasises the value of practising yoga, meditation, and mindfulness in order to encounter God and energy. These exercises enable us to access our inner consciousness and establish a connection with the divine energy that permeates our surroundings.

We can better comprehend our place in the cosmos and establish a connection with our inner selves by comprehending God's nature and the energy that permeates everything. Because in the present world, no culture desires its citizens to develop wisdom. All societies' investments are opposed by it.

People who are intelligent and sensible cannot be used or coerced into living a mechanical existence or acting like robots. They will cast doubt on the recognised institution. Since freedom comes with wisdom and no society wants to provide its people freedom for this reason, they will fight and speak out to defend their individuality and human rights.

It will be dangerous for the current system, dangerous for the people in power, and harmful for all forms of exploitation and oppression the moment people start using their own intelligence. However, a sensible man is like fire, preferring to perish than to live.

BIBLIOGRAPHY

- Bhagavad Gita by Silla Prabhu Pada, Bhaktivedanta Book Trust (BBT) publications.
- Kundalini, an untold story by Om Swami.
- Kundalini Tantra 1 by Satyananda Saraswati.
- Quantum Optics by DF Walls and Gerard J Milburn.
- Thermal Physics with Kinetic Theory, Thermodynamics and Statistical Mechanics by SC Garg, RM Bansal and CK Ghosh.
- Sri Garud Purana by Gita Press, Gorakhpur Hindi edition.
- Ranjit Chaudhri 112 Meditations for Self-Realisation: Vigyan Bhairava Tantra.
- Swami Vivekananda: The Complete Book of Yoga: Karma Yoga, Bhakti Yoga, Raja Yoga, Jnana Yoga.
- Om Swami-The Ancient Science of Mantras: Wisdom of the Sages.
- Pandit Ramnarayandat Shastri Panday: Mahabharata (Part 1-6), in Hindi, by Gita Press, Gorakhpur.
- Swami Vivekananda: Patanjali's Yoga Sutras.
- Swami Vivekananda: The Complete Book of Yoga: Karma Yoga.